HOW TO
BREAK 90

AN EASY, STEP-BY-STEP APPROACH FOR BREAKING GOLF'S TOUGHEST SCORING BARRIER

T. J. Tomasi, Ph.D., and Mike Adams
with Mike Corcoran

A Mountain Lion Book

McGraw·Hill

New York   Chicago   San Francisco   Lisbon   London   Madrid   Mexico City
Milan   New Delhi   San Juan   Seoul   Singapore   Sydney   Toronto

Library of Congress Cataloging-in-Publication Data

Tomasi, T. J.
    How to break 90 : an easy, step-by-step approach for breaking golf's toughest
scoring barrier / T. J. Tomasi and Mike Adams with Mike Corcoran.
       p.   cm.
    Includes index.
    ISBN 0-8092-9783-3 (hardcover) — ISBN 0-07-138559-2 (paperback)
     1. Golf.   I. Title: How to break ninety.   II. Adams, Mike, 1954–
III. Corcoran, Mike.   IV. Title.

   GV965.T62   2001
   796.352—dc21   00-64483

12 13 14 15 16 17 18 19 20 21 22   WFR/WFR   0

ISBN-13: 978-0-07-138559-6
ISBN-10:   0-07-138559-2

Cover design by Nick Panos
Front cover photograph copyright © Brian Bailey/Stone
Back cover photograph by Warren Ratz
Interior design by Max Crandall
Illustrations by Phil Franke

This book is printed on acid-free paper.

CONTENTS

INTRODUCTION

Congratulations. The book you're about to read is not another stupid golf book that starts out with five chapters on how to grip the club, and we're very pleased for you on that account. The reason this book doesn't start out like every other stupid golf book is that we know something about you already. We know you're pretty sure about how to hold the club. We know you get the ball airborne every time you swing at it—except on your putts, which become airborne only on special occasions. You're a good golfer, so we don't have to tell you stuff like keep your head down. (Which, by the way, we wouldn't tell you even if you weren't a good player.) You never sweat breaking 100 when you tee it up. You may even break 90 once in a while. And no fooling, when you break 90 that's good golf.

The reason you want to read this book is that you want to break 90 every time you tee it up, and that's what this book is going to help you do. We know how to help players like you because we've taught thousands of them at the Academy of Golf at PGA National, one of the world's finest golf schools and teaching facilities.

Since we already know a little something about your game, we've organized this book in a manner that is a little unusual for a golf book. We decided not to bombard you with fundamentals at the outset. Rather we packaged them all neatly for you and stuck them in the back of the book so you can refer to them on an as-needed basis.

The idea behind this book was to dive right into the things that will help you break 90. Things like how you think on the course and how you break down a hole so you can strategically plan your attack. The book starts with that and then evolves into a book that tells you how to play certain shots. All the while it reinforces your mind with ideas about how to analyze a situation and what tactics you should use.

We have spent the better part of our lives helping people play better golf. We know that the quest to break 90 is not something you take lightly. You want to be better at the game you spend a good amount of your free time playing. You want the respect of your friends and even the guys you don't like who play at your club. You want to be able to show up as your best buddy's member-guest and not embarrass yourself. After you've read this book, you'll no longer have to worry about that. You'll be the player everyone else is trying to beat. And it's a good feeling. We're happy to help fulfill your personal golf destiny. If you learn one thing from this book, let it be this: Learn to play golf with your head. That is where the low scores lie.

1

LEVEL
FIVES

Everyone who has ever played the modern game of golf has shared the common initial goal of shooting a score of less than 100. Many players—in fact, most players—never reach the goal of breaking 100 on a consistent basis. If you're reading this book, however, we're going to assume that you regularly shoot scores in the 90s and have set your sights on a new goal: shooting a score lower than 90 every time you tee it up.

We understand that this is an important goal for you and that it means something special. It means you'll have the respect of players of all levels, and for the first time in your experience as a golfer you'll feel like a *player*. When you can consistently break 90, you will feel like you can win your weekend matches and club tournaments. Your confidence will grow, and on days when everything is clicking you'll feel like you might even be able to shoot a score in the 70s. And you'll have every reason to feel so optimistic, because shattering the "90 barrier" is within your reach, and it is not as difficult as you might think.

Getting to Know Your Numbers

Let's begin with a short math lesson. There are 18 holes on a typical golf course. If you were to make a 5 on every one of those holes, you would shoot 90. It is not necessary to make a 5 on every hole, just to maintain an average per hole score of 5, something that is referred to as Level Fives.

Just in case that doesn't sound like good golf to you, allow us to mix a little history with your math: In the early 1900s, when golf was booming in both Great Britain and the United States, a score of bogey on a hole was considered superb golf for a nonprofessional. In fact, it was considered a pretty good score for a pro, too. The word bogey became synonymous with bad play with the inception of the concept of par. In the early days of golf, holes were not given par designations. The players simply tried to play the holes in the fewest possible strokes. Back in those days, players didn't sit around the grillroom saying, "I shot ten over par today," because the concept of par didn't exist. The term *par* came into use so it would be easier to compare the scores of tournament players. Par was determined to be the number of strokes that an *expert* player would require to hole out on a given hole. Then what we'll refer to as the Great Professional Golfer Bandwagon started to grip weekend golfers like a fever. Golf magazines and books used the professionals of the

> *Consider, if you will, that on a par-72 course you can bogey 17 of the 18 holes and still break 90.*
>
> — *Cliff McAdams*

day as an example of how the game should be played by all golfers. The problem with this, of course, was that golfers who played occasionally were suddenly comparing their performance to that of men who played the game for a living. It was like comparing your rose garden to Martha Stewart's: No matter how you looked at it, it just wasn't going to measure up.

The bandwagon mentality exists to this day, and the meaning of par hasn't changed: It's still the number of strokes an expert player will typically take on a given hole. Even Tiger Woods pars more holes than he birdies.

So now let us pose a question to you: If you consider par an average score, and par on a given golf course is 72, does that mean that you should shoot 72 if you play your typical game? If your answer is "Yes," then come summer you should pack your bags and head for the U.S. Open. More than likely, the answer is "No." And that's what your answer should be. However, if you're really hung up on the idea of shooting par, we have a suggestion for you: set par for a course at your level, not at the expert level. By setting your own Personal Par, you can do what you've always wanted to do—shoot a score under par.

SAY "HELLO" TO YOUR PERSONAL PAR

Every golfer on a quest to break 90 should use Level Fives as the measuring stick for success. Level Fives, or a score of 90, is your par. In other words, your Personal Par on each hole should be one more than the par indicated on the scorecard for that hole. This concept of Personal Par allows you to approach holes in a manner different from that of "regular" golf. Here's what we mean by that: A player is considered to have gotten the ball on the green in "regulation" when the ball rests on the green in two strokes less than whatever the par is for that hole. If the player takes two putts to get the ball in the hole, which is the norm, he'll have made a par. The truth of the matter is that a four is a four is a four, a five is a five is a five, and a three is a three is a three. In other words, it doesn't matter what combination of shots you play to make a score. It doesn't matter if you hit the green in "regulation." A chip and a single putt is just as good as two putts. It's all about the total number of strokes taken.

The difference between par and bogey is that the former represents perfect play and the other stands for good play, with a little margin here and there.

— James Braid

Since we're throwing the concept of traditional par right out the window, we may as well heave the idea of hitting a green in "regulation" right along with it. Here's how we'll do that.

If the scorecard indicates par for a hole is three, your Personal Par for the hole is four. You should consider your efforts successful if you get the ball on the green in two shots. If your ball is on the green in two shots, you've hit the green in Personal Par Regulation. If you put your tee shot on the green, all the better.

If the scorecard indicates par for a hole is four, your Personal Par for the hole is five. You should be aiming to get the ball on the green in three shots. If your ball is on the green in three shots, that's Personal Par Regulation for you.

If the scorecard indicates par for a hole is five, you should use a score of six as your Personal Par for that hole. Your ball-striking goal should be to get the ball on the green in four shots.

If you follow this logic and get your ball on each green in your Personal Par Regulation, you'll be able to take two putts on each hole to stay at Level Fives. The good news is that since you'll be hitting a lot of short approach shots and chip shots, you should be able to get quite a few of them close enough to the hole so that you can hole out in one putt. That's where you'll start to pick up the strokes that will get you under 90. Similarly, there's a good chance you'll get your ball onto a few greens in one shot less than Personal Par Regulation. If you take advantage of those opportunities by getting down in two putts, you can put yourself a few strokes below Level Fives.

You undoubtedly noticed we assumed you're going to be playing a lot of short approach shots, because reading this book is going to turn you into the smartest player in your Saturday foursome. Not only will you be hitting short approach shots, you'll be hitting them from the fairway, where you'll have maximum control over the shots.

USING PERSONAL PAR TO SET YOUR GAME PLAN FOR EACH HOLE

To borrow a term from football, employing Personal Par allows you to "break down" holes in a manner other than that to which you're accustomed. If a hole is less than 200 yards, your Personal Par for the hole is four and you should try to hit the green with your tee shot. If the hole is a par three on the scorecard, and measures 200 yards or more, you should plan to hit the green in two shots. There is a reason for this: generally speaking, the more loft on a club the easier it is to hit straight. Up to 200 yards, you're probably playing a club (a lofted fairway wood) with which you are very accurate. So even if you come up a little short, you'll be playing a shot from just in front of the green.

When the Personal Par Four is 200 yards or more, you're getting into a distance where you're more likely to miss the shot to the right or left of the green. Right and left of the green are usually the places where the trouble is. Sometimes the trouble is directly in front of the green, and if that's the case you can simply lay up short of it. When the hole is 200 yards or more, you want to avoid those trouble spots (bunkers and deep rough) to the sides of the greens, because these are the places that can prevent you from getting your next shot close to the hole. As a result, what you want to do is plan on using two shots to reach the green. This allows you to hit a shorter and more accurate club from the tee, and place it in a spot short of the green that will allow you to hit a short pitch shot from a good lie. You determine which club to hit from the tee based on the spot from which you'd prefer to play your second shot. If your favorite approach shot is from 40 yards, you should play a shot that leaves you 40 yards short of the green (as long as 40 yards short of the green is a viable option).

The same logic works for your Personal Par Five holes. If they are 350 yards or less, you should be able to comfortably reach them in two shots. You'll want to hit your "longest straight" club from the tee, i.e., the club with which you get the best combination of distance and accuracy. This might be your 3-wood, could be your 5-wood or even your 7-wood. The key is to focus on accuracy from the tee so you can play your longish approach shot from the fairway.

When the Personal Par Five is more than 350 yards, you're once again getting in that range that starts to overtax your ability to be accurate. So what do you do? You avoid the potential problem by not even bothering to attempt to reach the green in two shots. Rather, you play two short, straight shots that leave you within your comfort range for the approach. If, for example, you hit your 5-wood about 170 yards and fairly straight, you can do the following: Hit the 5-wood from the tee to make certain you get your tee shot in the fairway. There's never trouble in the fairway—at least not on a typical American golf course. If you hit a good shot, you'll have about 180 yards left

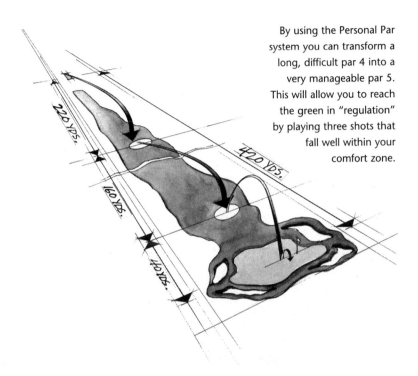

By using the Personal Par system you can transform a long, difficult par 4 into a very manageable par 5. This will allow you to reach the green in "regulation" by playing three shots that fall well within your comfort zone.

to the green on a 350-yard hole. Now you have a variety of options: You can hit your 5-wood again and get the ball close to the green. Or you can hit an even shorter club—say your 7-wood—and make it even more likely that you'll hit a straight shot. Either way, you'll have a wedge in your hand on the third shot, and, if you planned things properly, a good lie from which to play that wedge.

When your Personal Par Fives start creeping up toward 400 yards and up to 430 yards, you have to think smart on the tee. Play the hole in reverse to pre-plan your three shots. What length shot would you like to have into the green? You have to be honest with yourself. If your best shot is a 40-yard wedge shot, then play your first two shots so that you'll have that distance left to the green.

The above are just some examples of how you can use Personal Par to shape your game plan. We'll go into more specific and detailed plans of attack in a later chapter.

Avoiding the Big "Oh No"

Hopefully, you'll find many thoughts in this book that you'll carry with you out onto the course in your pursuit of breaking 90. Here are the first few thoughts we'd like you to adopt as rules. If you follow these suggestions every time you play, we promise you won't lose any momentum. More importantly, you'll completely avoid any of those moments when you watch the ball leave the clubface and mutter, "Oh *#!@#!"

Never Hit a Shot You Haven't Practiced

We've all been there. (Yes, even the authors of this book.) You hit a tee shot that slices a little bit and for your second shot you end up with trees between you and the green. A thought crosses your mind: If you could just punch a long iron on an arrow-straight line, maybe you could get the ball on the front of the green. The next time this happens to you, we recommend you ask yourself this question: How often do I practice hitting punch shots with long irons that fly straight as a rope? If the answer is "Never," don't attempt the shot. If you think this is a wimpy way to play golf, trust us. Even PGA Tour players don't try to play shots they don't practice. (Of course, they have an awful lot of time to practice, so they've practiced nearly every possible shot.) The point is this: You wouldn't turn the keys to your car over to a teenager who hadn't practiced driving with an adult, would you? And the reason is that the likely outcome would be an accident. If you try to play shots you haven't practiced, you'll get the same result. Stick to what you know and you'll stay away from marking snowmen on your scorecard.

Never Let One Shot Cost You Two

One of the great enemies in golf is frustration. The way frustration most commonly manifests itself is in two consecutive bad shots, the second caused by the seething frustration resulting from the first. Here are a few examples: You drive the ball into rough so deep that you can't really get any club on it other than a wedge. But you're playing pretty well, and you think you once read in a magazine that Arnold Palmer suggested you use a middle iron from heavy rough and play the ball back in your stance. So you do like Arnie said, but the club gets tangled up in the grass and your ball moves only a few feet and into an equally poor lie. You've gained nothing, and now in frustration you slash at the ball again, not wanting to "waste" a shot by playing a wedge out to the fairway. You get the same result. One poor shot turned into two.

Here's another example: Your ball is in a water hazard, but you can see the ball. It's sitting just below the water line, but the water is clear and you're quite certain that you saw Chi Chi Rodriguez pull this shot off in the Skins Game one year and save himself the penalty stroke incurred when taking a drop. So you take your pitching wedge and deliver a jackhammer blow at the ball, which promptly pops up in the air about an inch and then plops back into the water, deeper than it was before. Once again, you've followed a poor shot with another poor shot because you were trying to make up for the first one. When you're in trouble, the only smart thing to do is to get yourself out of trouble and set yourself up for a quality shot.

The best advice I can offer for playing a ball out of water is—don't.

— Tony Lema

Of course, the best way to avoid letting one bad shot cost you two strokes is to avoid the original bad shot altogether. That's not meant to sound smarmy. A lot of poor shots can be avoided simply by thinking them through before you play them.

Play Your Dominant Shot Pattern

Let's say that like most golfers, your tendency is to hit some type of slice or fade—a shot which curves from left to right. You arrive at the thirteenth tee and the hole is a dogleg to the left and there's out of bounds on the right. You conclude that the smart shot would be to hit a draw, a shot that will curve to the left right along with the fairway. So you aim down the right-hand side of the hole and you hit your usual fade. The ball goes out of bounds. Sam Snead said it best when he said, "You've got to dance with the one you brung with you," or words to that effect. What he means is if you have a dominant ball flight pattern— either left to right or right to left—don't try to fight it. And never aim at a spot where that ball flight will get you in trouble.

Be Smart When Carrying Water

This is a simple rule of thumb that you should refer to any time you're faced with a carry over water: If you can easily clear the water with a 5-iron, go for it. That doesn't mean you have to hit a 5-iron. You can hit a 3-wood if you want, but the distance shouldn't be any greater than what you carry with a 5-iron. If you miss the 3-wood slightly, you're still in business—the ball will still most likely carry the water. The flip side of this little rule is this: If you would need at least a 4-iron to carry the water, lay up. Stick to this rule consistently and you'll avoid wasting strokes on penalty shots and save a whole bunch of money on golf balls.

> *When your shot has to carry over a water hazard, you can either hit one more club or two more balls.*
>
> *— Henry Beard*

Keep the Ego in Check

Another seemingly simple and basic point, but this is probably the number one cause of mishaps during a round by an everyday player. Here's an example: You get on a tee and everyone else has a driver out. You feel more comfortable with a 5-wood, which doesn't go unnoticed by your boyhood chum Lefty. "Say," says Lefty. "I see you're gonna lay up on this one. What's wrong, feeling a little weak after that aerobics class this morning?" A lot of players would go back for the driver at this point, simply because they don't wish to give Lefty the satisfaction of feeling like he's right. The usual result: You overswing and hit a lousy shot. Here's our advice: Forget Lefty. Hit your 5-wood and win the hole.

WHICH TYPE OF 80S SHOOTER ARE YOU?

According the National Golf Foundation, a bunch of people who get paid to figure out stuff like this, the average score shot by the 25 million or so American golfers is 102. A mere 10 percent of all players consistently break 100. Only 5 percent break 90, and fewer than 1 percent break 80.

We've taught tens of thousands of golfers at our school, the Academy of Golf at PGA National in Palm Beach, Florida. We go over their rounds with them in detail as part of the curriculum, and we've come to the following conclusions.

In a typical round, golfers who consistently break 100 but fail to shoot lower than 90 hit only four fairways with their tee shots, take 40 putts, and usually don't make any birdies.

Golfers who consistently shoot lower than 90 typically hit six fairways with their tee shots, take only 32 putts, and commonly make no more than one birdie during the round.

At first blush, that probably doesn't seem like much of a statistical difference to you. Certainly it's not a difference so insurmountable that you can't close the gap. So what is it about the 80s shooters that sets them apart from the 90s shooters?

There are two types of 80s shooters. The first type is made up of better-than-average ballstrikers who don't have the time or inclination to work on their short game or think about course management. They could probably shoot in the 70s if they put their mind to it.

The other type of eighties shooter doesn't strike the ball much better than the guys who shoot ninety-five every week, but their overall game is enhanced by their deftness at those parts of the game which don't require as much physical talent. Those things are putting, chipping and sand play, course management, and brain management (keeping your emotions under control).

So, as you might have guessed by now, we're going to do two things during the rest of this book: Since you can break 100, we know you can get the ball airborne and hit it somewhat straight. That's why we're going to spend the majority of the book teaching you how to become a better scorer. The great news about this: Not only will you shoot lower scores and win more of your Saturday bets, but you'll drive your opponents bonkers in the process. Trust us on this: There's nothing sweeter than sitting in the grillroom with a cold beer while the guy you just took for $20 scratches his head and says, "I don't understand it. I hit the ball just as good as you do, but you beat me by ten shots. How do you do it?" The appropriate response is to shrug your shoulders.

The secondary goal of this book is to reinforce your knowledge of what makes for a fundamentally sound swing. Having a great swing is not the lone key to good scoring, but it's always useful to revisit the fundamentals. We'll cover the fundamentals so that you'll be able to fix your game when the occasional slump surfaces.

2

FINDING
THE
FAIRWAY

Next time you want to dazzle your playing partners with your brilliance, ask them this question: "Why do you think that closely mown patch of grass that creates a path to the green is called a fairway?" You'll more than likely stump them, because unlike everything else in golf, the meaning of the word is hardly obvious. The golf version of *fairway* is borrowed from a nautical term that describes a safe passageway through potentially dangerous waters. Now that you know that, you can understand why the term was adapted for golf. That short grass that outlines the recommended approach to a hole from the tee is there for a reason. If you keep the ball on the short grass, it stays out of harm's way. Most of the danger in golf lies off to the sides of holes in the form of trees, water, out-of-bounds, and ferocious animals with big pointy teeth. Okay, we made up that last part, but you get the picture.

> *The stories of bad scores rarely start with, "I ripped one right down the middle."*
>
> *— Colin Montgomerie*

The simplest way to make certain you play your second shot on any hole under optimal circumstances is to make sure you play the first shot onto the fairway. Since the tee shot sets the table for everything that comes after it, your first target is to get more tee shots in the fairway. This chapter is going to tell you how to do that, and at the end we'll throw in a few pointers on how to get a little extra distance on your tee shots, too.

THE SECRET TRUTH ABOUT GOLF

One of the trickle-down results of the Great Professional Golfer Bandwagon is what we'll refer to as the Great Big Driver Dichotomy. It works something like this: On a week-to-week basis, Tour players play on courses with very little rough. This means that for the most part they can swing away with the driver on almost every hole. On the rare occasions that they play a genuinely tough course, they are forced to *actually think* about their tee shots, and as a result they end up hitting the driver far less often than they are accustomed to. This is usually followed by post-round whining about how "the course took the driver out of my hands." So the Great Big Driver Dichotomy is that most Tour players feel the course should allow them to hit the driver on every hole because it's the club that gives them the greatest advantage on a hole. Sometimes, however, the golf course has something to say on the subject. Tour players don't like that, and as a result, weekend players don't either: If a Tour player is going to whine about it, then dammit, so is Joe Zilch.

Here's something wise to remember: No rule in golf dictates that you must hit your driver on every par four and par five. Nor is there any rule that says courses must be designed in a manner that allows every player to play to his or her strengths hole after hole. Golf is a diverse test. The truth of the matter is that you should hit your driver only a few times a round, if at all. Here's the reason why: Aside from your putter (which we definitely don't recommend playing from the tee), your driver has the least amount of loft of any club in your bag. (Just to be certain you're following us: Loft is the angle at which the club-face leans away from your target.) You probably already knew that, but you might not know that the amount of loft on a club and the chances you'll hit a straight shot are closely linked. The less lofted a club, the more difficult it is to hit straight. That's why you hit your short irons straighter than any other clubs in your set. The more loft the club has, the more backspin it puts on the ball. Backspin is your friend, because a ball with backspin generally flies straight and true.

Back in the old days, they didn't call it a driver. They referred to it as a "play club." In other words, it was the club you used to put the ball in play—maybe keep the ball in play. . . .

— Neal Lancaster

With the less-lofted clubs, such as drivers and long irons, there's a greater chance that you'll put sidespin on the ball. Sidespin is most definitely not your friend, since it causes the ball to curve. And when the ball curves it goes into those places where the animals with the pointy teeth live. Our recommendation is that you use your driver sparingly and opt instead for a 3-wood or even a 5-wood from the tee on most driving holes. The extra loft on these clubs will make two things happen. First, the ball will fly straighter, even if you mis-hit it. Second, since it will strike the ground at a steeper angle, it will roll less than a ball struck with a driver. That might sound like a bad thing, but it's not, because it means a ball that lands in the fairway has a better chance of staying in the fairway rather than bouncing off into the rough or trees.

The two baseline factors in determining which club to play from the tee on long holes are the length of the hole and the width of the fairway. Here are some guidelines for you to follow regarding club selection on Personal Par Fives and Personal Par Sixes.

If the hole is more than 400 yards in length and has a wide fairway, you can use your driver as long as there isn't trouble on the side of the hole your predominant shot pattern plays toward. In other words, if you consistently slice the ball (or maybe you like to think of it as a "power fade") and there is out-of-bounds on the right side of the hole, leave the driver in the bag and hit the 3-wood.

If the hole is more than 400 yards in length and has a narrow fairway, always use the 3-wood. How do you determine the definition of narrow? Certainly if you play the hole frequently and are in the woods more than half the time, it's narrow by your standards. Of course, other things factor into the definition of narrow—bunkers, water, etc. Since the width of some fairways is often inconsistent from tee to green, you want to focus on the area where you think your driver would land. If it's not wide enough to drive a tank through with your eyes closed (and without hitting anything), you shouldn't hit your driver. Once you've made the decision to hit the 3-wood, relax and make a good swing. Don't try to kill it because you think you need extra distance. You've made an intelligent decision to play for position. You still have to execute it. We wouldn't be at all surprised if you're always in the trees on this hole because you white-knuckle your driver because you think you need added length from the tee. Try to think of the combined length of two shots rather than just the length of the tee shot.

If the hole is 400 yards or less and has a wide fairway, our advice is to hit the 3-wood. The reasoning here is that since the hole is kind of short, about the only way you can really hurt yourself off the tee is to put the ball out of play. And your driver is the club you're most likely to put the ball out of play with by making a wild swing. Hit the 3-wood into the fairway and play one or two more clubs into the green.

If the hole is less than 400 yards long and has a narrow fairway, hit your 5-wood. If you don't have a 5-wood, ask your mother-in-law to buy you one for Father's Day or Mother's Day. If you're not a parent, adopt a kid. It's cheaper than buying a 5-wood.

On any hole that is a Personal Par Six, you can decide which club to hit from the tee based solely on the width of the landing area for the tee shot with each club. If the landing area for your driver is wide and doesn't have trouble on the side where your predominant ball flight will take you, go ahead and swing the driver. If you have trouble on "your" side of the landing area, hit the 3-wood. If the area is narrow overall, hit the 3-wood or the 5-wood. If it's super narrow, hit the 5-wood. The loss of distance isn't going to make a difference. And if the hole opens up after the tee shot, you can always hit the 3-wood on your second shot. Even if it doesn't, you'll still be close enough to the green to accomplish your mission after two solid 5-wood shots.

Like a lot of modern golfers, you may have a 7-wood in your bag. If you do, you should also consider it a viable alternative for your tee shots. Since many 7-woods are fitted with nearly 3-wood-length shafts you can hit the ball surprisingly far. We don't want to confuse you, and since we've mentioned the 3-wood, 5-wood, and 7-wood, you may be wondering which one you should use. The answer is whichever gives you the best combination of distance and accuracy, and exactly how precise you need to be with a given tee shot. If you hit the

3-wood straight, go for it. If you don't consistently hit the 3-wood straight and the hole is skinnier than a vegetarian, try the 5-wood. If you're not confident with that, try the 7-wood.

You'll notice we didn't mention playing long irons from the tee. The reason we didn't mention them is that you shouldn't play them from the tee or anywhere else. Take them out of your bag and forget they ever existed. If you don't carry a single digit handicap, you should not have a 1-iron, 2-iron, or 3-iron in your set. Have a garage sale, give 'em to your neighbor, use them as garden tools. Whatever you do, don't try to hit a golf ball with them. The lack of loft and small clubhead make them extremely difficult to hit consistently straight. The last thing you want to do is hit a crooked shot when you are attempting to play a smart shot into the fairway. The lofted fairway woods are much more user friendly. Stick with them.

> *The size and the looks of the woods alone are psychological aids and make these clubs easier to use, by the average player, than the long irons.*
>
> *— Tommy Armour*

Becoming the Smartest Player in Your Foursome!

In giving you the above guidelines for selecting a club from the tee on Personal Par Fives and Personal Par Sixes, we described them as *baseline* factors because you need a place from which to start to assess your shot. Now we're going to toss out the variables you should consider. Some of this stuff is really cool, so pay attention. Knowing it isn't going to win you a Nobel Prize, but what the heck, you only paid eleven bucks for this book. You'll win that back your first time out after reading this section.

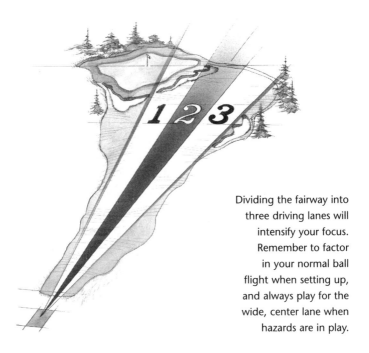

Dividing the fairway into three driving lanes will intensify your focus. Remember to factor in your normal ball flight when setting up, and always play for the wide, center lane when hazards are in play.

Divide the Fairway into Driving Lanes

This little trick falls into the category of "oldie but goodie." You've probably seen it in the magazines a couple hundred times. The idea behind it is that you want the lanes to be of equal width, and you never want the ball to curve more than two lanes. That means you want to use a club that is going to give you that amount of curve or less. The trick here is that the width of the lanes depends on the overall width of the fairway in the landing area. The narrower the lanes, the straighter the shot you need to hit.

Play for the Widest Lane

Okay, now pay attention. The lanes you're visualizing are *straight lanes*. They don't curve with the contours of the fairway.

The middle lane is almost always going to be the widest, but not always. Check out the pattern of the fairway in the landing area and figure out which one is the widest. Play for that one.

Play Your Dominant Shot Pattern

If you're lucky enough to hit a fade or a draw every time you play a shot, don't ever try to fight that. You're not going to face too many situations where you absolutely must hit the ball with a certain type of curve to it. And for those situations when you do, we'll tell you later in the book how to play them. Even if your shot pattern is inconsistent, you probably have a dominant shot pattern. Go with that. If you're so inconsistent that you never know where the ball is going, you're probably not breaking 100. You should be reading a different book.

Never Aim for Danger

If your dominant pattern is right to left, and there's a shark-infested pond on the right side of the fairway, do not aim at the pond unless there are hurricane-force winds blowing from right to left. If you aim at that pond, sure as shootin' you're going to hit it straight. It's just one of those things we can't explain but always happens. If the pond is on the right and the widest lane is in the center, and you have a lane on the left, hit a club that will probably put you in the center and at worst will put you in the left lane.

Play a Draw from the Left Side of the Tee

Keeping the above in mind, if your shot is a right to left mover you'll want to tee up on the far left side of the markers. Generally speaking this will place the ball slightly above your feet and encourage the draw ball flight. The reason for this is that most teeing areas are slightly pitched, with the highest part in the center. This is done by design so water can run off. Even if you play at a muni where the tees are as flat as western Texas, teeing up on the left side will effectively create more room for you in the fairway.

Play a Fade from the Right Side of the Tee
Why? Just read the above and imagine the opposite.

Trouble to the Left—Tee It Slightly Lower
By teeing the ball slightly lower than you're accustomed to, you'll feel compelled to make more of a downward swing at the ball, that is, the club will come into the ball moving across the target line from right to left. This type of swing normally results in a fade.

Trouble to the Right—Tee It Slightly Higher
Not so high that you pop it up, just slightly higher. This will promote a more inside-to-out swing, with the clubhead moving across the target line from left to right. This type of swing normally produces a draw.

The true strategic mindset of managing your tee shots is to view them as the opening shot in 18 separate battles you fight during a round. Each hole is a battle unto itself. It has a clear beginning and end. Once each battle is completed, you can't do anything to change it. And just because you win one doesn't mean you can assume you'll win the next one. All this is done within the larger framework of winning the war—shooting the final score you want.

The first move in each of your battles is the tee shot, but where to place the tee ball is not your first decision. To arrive at that determination you must play a quick game of connect-the-dots in reverse. We'll make some assumptions here, namely that you're familiar with the course and you know the position of the hole on the green either by eyeballing it or using one of those little diagrams of the green some courses and clubs make available to players. (If the course you're playing provides one of these green diagrams, refer to it before you hit your tee shot.)

Once you know where the hole is cut on the green, you should determine from what distance and angle you want to play your approach shot to the hole. Once you figure out that point, plot your way back to the tee identifying the spots from where you'd like to play, keeping in mind the lane strategies described above.

As you start to assemble this pattern of dots or points, there are a few things you should consider other than the obvious goal of avoiding hazards and trees.

You want to play as many shots as possible from level ground. Any time the ball is above or below your feet it dramatically increases the difficulty of a shot. The same goes for lies that are downhill (your body tilting toward the target) and uphill (your body tilting away from the target). If you have a choice between playing to Position A, which is 20 yards closer to your eventual goal but offers uneven terrain, and Position B, which is 20 yards farther back but with level ground, opt for Position B.

Always factor in the two variables that make up the total distance of a shot, namely carry and roll. The carry portion of the equation is affected by the wind and the lie of the ball. Obviously, shots played into the wind do not carry as far, and shots played downwind carry farther. As far as the lie is concerned, if the ball is sitting down in the grass, you're not going to make clean contact with it. You have to be aware of that and realize the ball is not going to carry as far.

How much the ball rolls is determined primarily by the club with which it's struck. The higher a shot flies, the less it will roll when it hits the ground. This is because of the angle of descent it takes toward the ground. There are more variables with roll than with carry. A ball hit into the wind will roll less when it hits the ground because the wind accentuates the normal backspin. Shots hit downwind will run substantially more than shots hit in windless conditions. The downwind neutralizes the backspin and creates a sort of knuckleball effect. When the ball hits the ground—even the green—it is going to scamper along quite a bit. How much depends on the loft of the club you're using—the more loft, the less roll. But even with a wedge, the ball is going to run between 10 and 15 yards when it lands.

Course conditions also impact on roll. If the ground is hard from lack of rain, the ball is going to run more no matter how much the greens superintendent waters the course. When the course is wet, the ball will not roll as much as it does under normal conditions.

Preparing to Play the Tee Shot

If you watch the pros play on television, you've probably noticed that almost to a player they take a practice swing before every shot. Chances are you do, too, but are you accomplishing anything with your practice swing? You may have heard before about how the practice swing should be a rehearsal for the swing you're about to make. This is true, but it's not just a physical rehearsal—it's a dry run for your mind as well. Here are a few suggestions for how to get the most out of your practice swings.

First, make your practice swing facing the target. You may see some pros do otherwise, but they have a set purpose in mind for doing so, and it won't do you any good to try to copy every individual little wrinkle you see from tour players as a group. By taking your practice swings in the direction of the target, you get all of your physical and mental energy focused at your target. That may sound a little touchy-feely, but trust us, it helps. If you take your practice swing facing a house or a water hazard, how is that possibly going to help you?

While taking your practice swing, visualize the shot you want to play with the ball flying all the way to the target. If your mind sees the shot for you before you hit it, there's a better than good chance it will direct your body to reproduce the practice swing when you actually swing at the ball.

Finally, always swing the club at the speed you want to swing it during the real thing, and make the same shaped swing you want to make when putting the ball into play. If your normal shot is a draw and you normally swing a little inside-out, then do that during the practice swing. The closer the warm-up swing is to the real thing, the better your chances of making the swing you want when it counts.

The Power Ball

We aren't crazy even though we spend an awful lot of time in the sun. We realize that hitting longer tee shots can have a positive effect on your game in terms of your emotional satisfaction and your actual score. We know this for a fact, because at our schools we occasionally take superhigh handicappers out for playing lessons and let them finish the hole after we hit their tee shots for them. When we do this, players who couldn't break 100 if it were a pane of glass and they had a brick have no difficulty in shooting a score of less than 100.

As we said, we're not crazy, so we're going to spend a few pages talking about the subject of how to add distance to your shots. Before we do that, however, let's make a deal: We'll tell you how to hit longer shots if you promise never to let your quest for distance supersede your quest to break 90. For you to live up to your end of the bargain, when you're on the course you have to focus on being a strategic player. Take these power lessons and work them into your game on the practice tee and in practice rounds. Work them into your game slowly. Don't finish this chapter and assume you can bust every tee shot 265 yards. Don't lose your objectivity about your own game.

Enough of the caveats, then. Let's get down to business.

In order to add distance to your game, you have to grasp the concept behind a more powerful swing. It's a concept we can explain using everyday images, so it's not like reading one of those nutty books that will overwhelm you with ideas like how your body is the perfect golf machine and a bunch of crap about levers and winches and pulleys and stuff. To understand how to generate power, all you have to do is think about a simple, ordinary spring.

So close your eyes and visualize a metal spring. (Kind of tough reading with your eyes closed, isn't it?) Now, let's say one end of that spring is anchored to something such as a board. Now take your hand and grab the loose end of the spring and begin to turn it in the direction that makes it tighter. Keep turning and turning until it's as tight as it can go. Now, let go. Amazing! The spring unwinds without your doing a thing once you let go. This experiment isn't going to win you the county science fair, but if you understand what just happened, you understand how power is generated in the golf swing. More importantly, if you understand that visualization, you're capable of generating more power in your golf swing.

The practical application of this spring analogy works like this: The spring had a fixed end because it needs resistance against which it can coil; in your golf swing your right foot and leg act as the fixed end during your backswing. The rest of your body turns around your fixed point. The farther a body part is from the fixed point, the more it has to turn to be wound as tightly as possible. In other words, that means your shoulders have to turn the farthest. Your hips have to turn, too, but not as

To get into a more powerful position at the top of your swing, coil your body by making your shoulders and hips rotate as far as they can.

far, since they are closer to the fixed point. The idea is to turn your hips and shoulders as far as you possibly can—you can't turn too far. When you've turned as far as you can, you've loaded the spring with energy.

When your swing is fully loaded with energy at the top of your backswing, the maximum amount of energy is at the core of the spring—the part closest to the resistance. That means your hips have the most energy stored up in them. Your arms—and by extension the club—have some energy in them, but mostly they are going to react to the unleashing of the energy in the hips. When your hips start to uncoil at the beginning of the downswing, there's a delayed response from the shoulders and arms. In other words, when your hips start turning toward the target, your shoulders and arms do not join in simultaneously. In fact, there is a split second when your hips are turning one way (toward the target) while your shoulders and arms are moving the opposite way (still turning away from the target). This happens because your shoulders and arms have a longer way to go, but your hips can't wait for them to get there to unleash the energy. That delayed response is sometimes referred to as "the pause at the top."

Once your shoulders and arms begin to uncoil, they pick up speed rapidly and eventually catch up to your hips. The fastest moving part in this whole spring action is the thing farthest from the fixed point—the clubhead. And the faster that clubhead is moving, the farther that ball is going to fly.

Making It Work

The sequence of movements in a powerful swing is critical to success. Use the following set of checkpoints to help you get the sequence down pat.

Starting your backswing: Your right leg is the point you want to be steadiest. If you start your backswing by keying on turning your right hip away from the target, you'll get most of your weight shifted onto your right leg. Specifically, you want it on the inside of your right leg. With your weight distributed in this manner, that leg will be like a steel girder. So your trigger thought is this: Turn your right hip away from the target.

The shoulders follow: Once you start to turn your hips, your shoulders will follow. It's nearly impossible to turn your hips even a little bit without turning your shoulders, too. And since you're going to try to turn your hips as much as you can, your shoulders will surely follow. Your arms will swing right along with the turning of the shoulders. A quick note about how far your shoulders should turn: If you watch golf on television, you hear a lot about getting the club "to parallel." What they mean is that at the top of the backswing the shaft of the club is parallel with the ground. Quite often this notion of "getting parallel" is held up as a goal you must achieve in order to hit the ball a long way. That idea is nonsense. When Dan Pohl played on the PGA Tour in the 1980s he was one of the longest hitters out there, and he barely got the club past being perpendicular to the ground in his backswing! "Parallel" is nothing more than a reference point—a road sign on a road you know like the back of your hand. And since you don't have eyes in the back of your head (unless you're our mother), you cannot accurately detect the position of the shaft while you're swinging. A much easier way to gauge the amount of shoulder turn you achieve is to use your left shoulder as your reference point. Your shoulder turn is at maximum capacity when your left shoulder is tucked underneath your chin and you feel you can't stretch it another fraction of an inch.

One final thought on making your shoulder turn. When you turn your body away from the ball, you want to think about making a "level" turn. What that means is keeping your hips and your shoulders level with the ground. This doesn't mean you have to go out into the workshop, dig out your level, and tie it to your hips when you play golf. Making a level turn is more about what you *don't* want to do in your swing, that is, you don't want to have any sort of detectable lean toward or away from the target. The most common way of communicating this idea seems to be "make a level turn," which for our money seems a little too precise and creates another of those situations where you can't really tell if you're achieving it because you're looking at the ground. It's probably a lot easier just to think, "Don't lean." (The problem with leaning, by the way, is that it starts your arms and the club moving up and down in a chopping action. That's bad. You want them swinging "around" rather than "up and down.")

Making the transition: Hang on, baby, the payoff is coming. When you reach the top of your swing you've actually reached the decisive moment of your golf swing. The climax comes at impact, but the critical moment of influence occurs when your backswing ends and your downswing begins.

The danger at the top of your swing lurks in the battle between your instincts and your faith in your swing. Your instinct at the top of your swing is to deliver a hammer blow at the ball. Here we go, baby! We're going to crush this one! Tear the damned cover right off that stupid ball! And so forth. Sadly, the cover is seldom torn off as a result of this thinking. It's the same instinct that overtakes the muscle man when he tries to ring the bell at the Test of Strength at the county fair. He swings the mallet up over his head and as he readies to bring it down, he tenses the muscles in his hands and arms and squeezes the handle of the mallet for all he's worth. He feels strong. Observe me, puny weaklings! I am strong man! And he strikes at the thingy that launches the ringer upward, and it gets about halfway to the bell. Why doesn't the strong man have the stuff to make the bell go ding? Because he doesn't know that a powerful blow *cannot be forced, it must be allowed to happen.* In this case, there is literally power in knowledge.

When the strong man tries to foist his own sense of power upon the situation, he interrupts the natural momentum that will lead to a powerful moment of impact. Think about the word momentum and how it is commonly used. It is always used in combination with words such as *gain* and *build up.* A series of things create momentum, but a single thing can stop it.

By the time you've reached the top of your swing, you've created some serious momentum in terms of clubhead speed. It may not seem like the club is moving fast, but you've allowed it to gradually pick up speed. Of course, it's hard to think about anything being gradual when the whole swing takes place in the blink of an eye. But, relatively speaking, gradual is precisely the way to describe the accumulation of clubhead speed. There is really only one way that this creation of momentum can be interrupted. And, of course, that way is the very thing that feels most instinctive—to grab on tight and tense the muscles. (Just one of the many reasons golf is the game you hate to love.)

> *Many shots are spoiled at the last instant by efforts to add a few more yards. This impedes rather than aids the stroke.*
>
> *— Bobby Jones*

The important question here when all is said and done is how do you allow the buildup of power to continue uninterrupted? Answering that question and understanding that question are simple; it's getting yourself to actually do it that's the tough part. The way you let the power process continue is to begin your downswing from the ground up. In other words, when you reach the moment when you've turned your shoulders back as far as you can, don't immediately uncoil them. Instead, start the process with your hips. Specifically, your left hip. Start the downswing by thinking about turning your left hip toward the target. This will allow your "spring" to unwind in the proper sequence and allow the clubhead to continue to gain momentum. When you lead with your hips, you give your upper body (shoulders) a chance to have that extra split second they need to complete their windup and to allow the clubhead to smoothly change directions.

Not everyone feels comfortable keying on the left hip. If you're a right-sided person, that is, everything feels better to you on the right, then it's equally useful to think about "firing" your right hip toward the target as well. Either way, you accomplish the mission.

If you make it through the transition part of the swing with the sequence of body movements occurring in the correct order, you're halfway home to longer shots. Coordinating the sequence of body movements with the speed of the body movements is the second half of the equation.

Cruise Control

Without understanding how to moderate the speed of your body you'll never hit maximum clubhead speed. How many times have you hit a poor drive and had someone in your group say, "Wow, if you swung any faster you'd come out of your shoes." Or perhaps, "Hey, Speedie, slow it down a little bit." If the person who says that to you is someone whose eye you trust, then it's worth thinking about. (If it's someone who can't break 120 on a good day, wait until he's not looking and let the air out of the tire on his cart.) Even though you hate to hear those admonishments from your buddies, they are onto something. Generally speaking, it's not the speed of your swing they're noticing, but your lack of tempo. The speed of your swing and the tempo of your swing are related, but they are not the same thing. Speed is something you don't have much control over—it's the cumulative effect we described with the spring analogy. You can stay out of its way, but you can't control it much. Speed is how fast the club is moving at any given moment. Tempo is the consistency of the pace of your body movements. Ideally, you want clubhead speed to be at its highest at the moment of impact, but that can happen only if you moderate your tempo. The speed of your conscious body movements should stay consistent throughout your swing.

This concept usually raises a few eyebrows. After all, don't you have to increase the speed at which your body is moving to increase the speed at which the club is moving? The answer is no, and we'll give you another little science fair project to demonstrate: Take a common bit of hardware known as a washer. You know, the circular thing with the hole in the middle—the hardware store's version of a donut. Some are made of rubber and some are made of metal. You'll want a metal one for this project. Now take a piece of string about 12 inches long or so. Tie the washer to one end of the string. Now take the other end of the string and tie it to your index finger. Make it snug enough that you'll be able to twirl the washer around without it flying off your finger. Once you've secured the string to your finger, start moving the finger in a tight circular motion so that the washer starts to twirl around your finger. Notice that the washer moves slowly at first and then picks up speed as the string shortens. In fact, it picks up speed without your increasing the speed at which you move your finger. Additionally, if you continue to wind and unwind the string around your finger, you'll notice the more "quiet" you keep your finger (the less side-to-side movement you make with it), the faster the washer will go. The washer is gaining speed due to the consistent pace of the movement at the center of its power source. The washer is not at the center of the power source, but the consistent flow from the power source lets it build up speed in an uninterrupted fashion.

Now, class, using this analogy, what part of the golf club is represented by the washer? Did you say the clubhead, Pat? That is correct. And the string represents the shaft of the club, and your index finger represents your body. So the end point here is that the tighter and more evenly paced the turn of your body is, the faster that clubhead is going to move. The key thing here is that *the clubhead doesn't start out travelling at maximum speed. It picks up speed as it travels.* If it starts the swing too quickly or in an out-of-control fashion, it cannot gain speed—there's not enough time to recover. The swing is over in a second. If your tempo—the pace of your body movements—is uneven at any time, you will either block momentum or disrupt it.

Here are rules of the road, so to speak, when it comes to keeping an eye on your body speed limit.

First things first: The tempo of your swing refers to the collective speed of all the body parts in motion at a given time. Your arms don't have a different tempo than your shoulders or hips. It's a package deal.

The eventual outcome of things (the flight of the ball) is dramatically influenced by what happens during the first 18 inches of the backswing. If you can start the club back slowly, you're in good shape. If you whip the club back frantically, you've got big problems because you'll never be able to gain control of the club. (Not to mention you'll probably have yanked it way too far inside the target line.) One of the best swing keys ever thought up is three simple words to describe the beginning of your backswing: *Low and slow.* That pithy advice means to keep the club low to the ground as long as you can, that is, until your arms have no choice but to start swinging upward. Concentrating on making a level turn will help. The slow part just means you don't have to be in a hurry. Give things time to build. If you start out with slow body movements, they are easy to maintain. If you start out with quick body movements, those are very difficult to maintain without losing control.

The top of your swing is not only important in terms of sequence of movements, but pace of movements as well. This is the place where you're most likely to screw up your tempo, and it's for the same reasons that you're likely to mess up the sequence. The urge to kill. You feel it's time to quicken the pace because it doesn't feel like things are happening fast enough. If you focus on starting the downswing by leading with the lower body as we advised earlier, you should be in good shape. But swing keys have only a limited warranty: They wear out quickly and you need a replacement. A good replacement key in this situation is to think about ballroom dancing with your sweetie, even if you have two left feet. Trust us, it actually works if you hum to yourself in a dance cadence of one . . . two . . . three . . . one . . . two . . . three . . . one . . . two . . . three, etc. Start your swing at "one," transition to the downswing at "two," and arrive at impact at "three."

If by nature you do things quickly, or slowly, you're going to swing the golf club the same way. Forcing yourself to an opposite extreme is rarely going to work because it's too contrary to your basic instincts or impulses. . . .

— Jack Nicklaus

So now you know that keeping the same pace to your body movements is important, but what exactly is that pace? Even a monkey could tell you that everyone doesn't swing at the same pace. (In fact, monkeys do tell you whenever you watch golf on television.) Let's take a look at a few classic examples from the professional ranks—Tom Watson, now a PGA Senior Tour member, and Colin Montgomerie, the Scot who is currently one of the world's finest players.

If you watched Watson you'd say that compared to most players he seems to have a quick pace to his swing. In comparison, you'd have to say Montgomerie appears to swing at a slower pace. In both cases, you'd be right—the pace of Watson's body movements is much quicker than that of Montgomerie. So what's up with Watson? Should he slow down? If he had a slower tempo, would he have won ten British Opens instead of five? Actually, what you see when comparing Watson and Montgomerie (or any two golfers, for that matter) is that the pace of the player's swing is matched very closely by the natural pace at which he does other things. In other words, the pace of the body swing matches the person's natural speedometer. Watson, for example, walks quickly between shots and thinks quickly on his feet. He makes his club selection and goes through his pre-shot routine as fast as any professional ever. Montgomerie, on the other hand, operates at a slower pace. He lopes along between shots—not slowly, but not as fast as Watson—and he is more deliberate in preparing to play a shot. The story here, friend, is that your pace of swing should match the way you walk, talk, think and breathe. And that idea of swinging the club "low and slow?" Well, "slow" means whatever slow feels like to you. The key if you do things quickly is to focus on *maintaining pace throughout your swing.*

POWER OUTAGES

All the stuff we just told you is all you need to know if you want to add length to your shots. There are other things you can do to pick up a yard or two, but they're also the kind of things that can really screw you up if you start messing with them. So we're not going to worry about them in this book. What we do want to address before moving on to the next chapter, however, is what to do when you suddenly and mysteriously start to lose distance on your tee shots (and other shots as well). So if you hit a slump where you're consistently hitting your tee shots 10–15 yards shorter than you normally do, here's the maintenance check list to go through:

Applying the Grip of Death

Tension is the single biggest killer of distance in golf. Here's why: All of that stuff about the spring, the winding and unwinding, and the energy is based upon the club being able to react to what your body is doing. Your body's ability to do its job is predicated on its being tension-free. You can't get the proper amount of windup (turn) if you're resisting that turn. The only source of resistance should be in your legs. Tension in the upper body is common among poor players but can occasionally creep into anyone's game. The place where that upper-body tension usually starts is in your hands. Specifically, what we're talking about here is squeezing the club too tightly. So if your drives start coming up lame, check your grip pressure. You should never feel like you're "squeezing" the club. Just hold it hard enough to prevent it from flying out of your hands. If you can feel any tension at all in your forearms, you're squeezing too tightly.

The Hallowed Reverse Pivot

We talked about the importance of this a little earlier. The ugliest and one of the most common faults in golf is something called a reverse pivot. Who knows why so many golfers fall into the category of those who make this mistake, but here's what happens: In a fundamentally sound swing, you start out with your weight evenly distributed between both legs. When you start your backswing, the majority of your weight shifts onto the inside of your right leg. When you begin your downswing, the weight is shifted onto your left leg.

In the reverse pivot, the player does the complete opposite during his swing. During the backswing, the player actually shifts his weight into the front leg. And since this is happening at the same time the club is being swung back, the player contorts himself into a bizarre tropical-bird-like stance and finds himself leaning toward the target. The result of this ill-fated tango with self is that no coiling action occurs. No spring. No power. No nothing. In the downswing, the player has to shift his weight to his rear leg to prevent falling over. The net result of all of this is that the poor guy is falling away from the target as he nears impact. This is a description of a severe case of a reverse pivot. You're a pretty fine player, so in your case what you want to check for is a minor case of the reverses, i.e., maybe you're not tipping toward the target, but maybe your weight shift isn't happening. Maybe you're keeping your weight centered and neutral rather than the necessary right-left shift. Check it out by keying on shifting your weight onto your right hip as you start the club back. If you start nailing the ball, you've fixed your problem.

Starting Down from the Top

Another really hideous move that pulls the plug on power is known as casting from the top. This is the term used to describe a downswing that begins from the top (arms and shoulders) instead of the bottom (hips). It's a superweak move. We've covered the proper sequence of events in detail earlier in this chapter. If your shots are feeling weak, refer to that good stuff.

Failing to Keep Your Feet on the Ground

Check your feet. If the tips of your shoes are perpendicular to the target line, you're limiting your hip turn. Flare both feet out a little bit—the left foot toward the target and the right foot

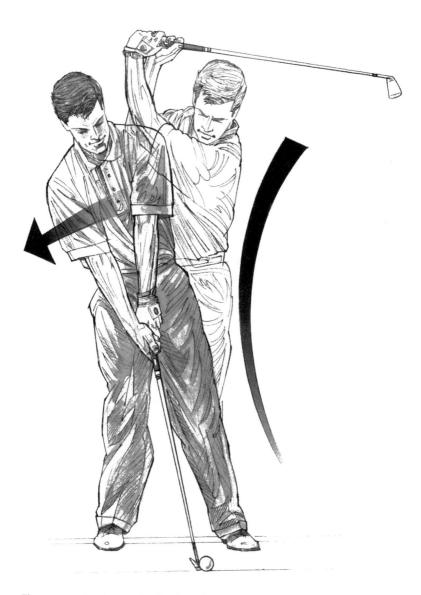

The reverse pivot is a motion in which the body's weight stays on the front side during the backswing, then shifts to the back side on the downswing. This is exactly the opposite of what happens in a good swing.

In a good swing, the weight shifts to the front side on the downswing, with the head behind the ball and the hands slightly behind or even with the ball.

away from the target. This will help you make a bigger turn away from and through the ball. The other thing to check on is your footwork during the swing. You see a lot of golfers who pick their heels way up off the ground, the left heel on the backswing and the right heel in the downswing. The left heel move isn't bad as long as you kick your left knee toward your right knee, shifting the weight onto your right leg. If you kick your knee out toward the ball, you'll lose your balance.

The right heel coming off the ground in the downswing is a bigger problem. Keep that sucker anchored on the ground or you'll create an energy leak in your swing.

A Tried and True Classic: You're Trying to Kill It

Sound too simple or lame that a good player like you might hit a stretch where you fall into that oldest of all swing vices, trying to crush the ball? Well, it happens. Your mind is a powerful tool in everything you do, and golf is no exception. If you purposely try to kill the ball, it's not going to work. Not consistently, anyway. As the great pitcher Orel Hersheiser always said, "You cannot fail when you focus on execution instead of results." Turn and tempo. They're the keys. If you want to hit it hard, zone in on those two things.

3

BECOMING DEADLY
WITH YOUR
SHORT IRONS

When you make the choice to become a strategic golfer, you place a lot of emphasis on improving the accuracy of your short irons. The reason for this is that since you're frequently going to hit something other than your driver off the tee, you're going to be playing some layup shots on longer holes. After you've successfully executed that layup shot, you're going to have a short iron in your hand. The short irons are the scoring clubs in golf—the clubs you should and can expect to hit close to the hole. Since the short irons have the most loft on the clubface and the shortest shafts, they are perfect for hitting deadly accurate shots. The great degree of loft almost ensures you'll hit a straight shot if you set up to the ball properly (we'll cover that in a bit), and the shorter shaft allows for a much shorter and controlled swing. That means it's less likely you'll make a mistake in your swing mechanics.

Now that you're a strategic golfer—more specifically, a strategic scorer—you have to familiarize yourself with all the nuances of becoming a great short-iron player. The first part of becoming a marksman with your short irons takes place on the practice ground. You didn't think you were going to get away with breaking 90 without a little bit of time on the practice ground, did you?

Digging in the Dirt

Legend has it that Ben Hogan once said that the secret to good golf was in the dirt. What he meant, of course, was that the real secret lay in hitting a lot of practice shots. We're not crazy enough to think you've got nothing better to do with your time than practice your golf game. (After all, you've got to actually play golf and then sit around drinking beer and talking about it, and that takes some time, too.) What we want to ask of you is one really good practice session so you can nail down precisely how far you hit the following clubs: 7-iron, 8-iron, 9-iron, pitching wedge, and sand wedge.

This practice session has a few requirements in order for you to gain the maximum benefit from it. First, you need a dry day without any significant wind. Second, you need an empty practice ground. Third, you need a buddy to help you out. (Maybe a son or daughter who's interested in the game will help.)

To get an empty practice ground it's best to shoot for really early in the day. If you belong to a private club, this might be a little easier. If you don't, check with the pro at your public course or practice range and see when it's most likely to be empty. You'll want to hit the shots from a flat lie with the grass mown at fairway length. In a lot of places, the wind dies down toward the end of the day as the sun sets. This is also a good time to find an empty practice range, so you might want to shoot for a late afternoon. You're going to need 100 balls. If they're new range balls, that should be okay. If they've got nothing but old beaters at the place, start your own collection of balls you find in the woods. (If you play at the same course our friends do, it'll take you only about a week to find 100.) It's important that you have 100 decent balls to use, because you want them to resemble the kind you use when you play. If you use a bunch of old, dead range balls, you're not going to get a true reading out of this exercise.

So now you've got your 100 balls and your five clubs, a good spot on a good day, and a helper. You'll need one more thing, some sort of marker or target you can hit toward. We suggest you use some old towels. You'll need nine of them. If you don't have old towels, maybe some old shirts, or some construction cones you stole off the interstate when they were building the new overpass. Anything is good, as long as you can carry them without too much trouble and you'll be able to see them from the spot you're going to use as your "tee."

Arm yourself with your towels or whatever, and pace off 80 yards from the spot from which you're going to hit the balls. Drop the first marker at 80 yards. Then drop one every 10 yards until you get to 160 yards. When you're done you'll have markers at 80, 90, 100, 110, 120, 130, 140, 150, and 160 yards. So far you're doing well. Wait, we almost forgot! You'll need two more things: a writing implement and a piece of paper. Stick the pencil and paper in your helper's hand and send him or her packing. You're going to start with the shortest club, the sand wedge. So tell the helper to head out to between the 80- and 100-yard markers and stand off to the side. What you want your helper to do is note the carry of each of the 20 balls you hit with the sand wedge. That means your helper should be watching for where the ball strikes the ground, not where it runs to (although with a sand wedge it shouldn't run too far).

Getting Your Body Aimed Correctly with Your Short Irons

One element of your short game that deserves specific attention is the idea of getting your body aimed correctly with the short irons because of the difference in the shape of the swing with the short irons. The swings you make with the other clubs in your bag tend to be more on the "flat" side, with the club swinging "around" your body. With the short irons, the club is swung more "upright," or more up and down, instead of around your body. There is a reason for this: The shaft of the club is shorter, so you have to stand closer to the ball. And since you have to stand closer to the ball, the smart guys who design golf clubs for a living make it so that the shafts of the short irons come out of the clubhead at a more upright angle. (This property of a club—that angle at which the shaft protrudes from the clubhead—is referred to as "lie.") They do this so you don't have to bend over too far from the waist and slouch your shoulders, things that would make golf a very uncomfortable game. Those two things—the fact that you're standing closer to the ball and the lie angle—create the need for a few adjustments when you're lining up your shot.

Any time you line up to play a shot, the process begins with the selection of a target. Things are no different with your short irons. You select your target standing behind the ball and looking directly at the target. (Your target is the place you want the ball to hit the ground, not where you want it to finish up after it stops running along the ground.) You don't pick your target standing to the side of the ball from the position in which you're going to make your swing. This is especially important with your short irons, because the closer you get to the target the more difficult it is to get your body set correctly. The reason for this is that you have to make an adjustment in the position of the ball in relation to your body with your short irons.

Since your swing is more upright and you're standing closer to the ball with a short iron, the club is going to come in contact with the ground much earlier in your downswing than it would with a fairway wood or a 4-iron, for example. This means that you need to move the ball farther back in your stance than you place it for those longer shots. (If you don't, you're going to hit an awful lot of fat shots, and a few thin ones, too.) Simply put, you must have the ball in the same position at which the club is going to reach the bottom of its swing arc. The sneaky little thing here, however, is that most of the written and teaching references to ball position talk about the ball in relation to your *feet*. And that, friends, doesn't do you any good, because your feet are naturally going to move a little closer together when you stand closer to the ball. What that means is moving your reference point. You need your reference point to be fixed, not moving with every shot. For that reason, we're going to encourage you to use your chest as the reference point for ball position. No matter how far apart you move your feet, your chest is not going to expand and contract. With your short irons, you should place the ball even with the center of your chest. That will put the ball in the position you need it to coincide with the bottom of the swing arc.

> *Most of the things that contribute to a bad shot in golf occur before you begin your backswing.*
>
> *— Jim Flick*

Now you may be wondering what in the world the position of the ball at address has to do with how you aim your body at address. The answer is that having the ball in the center of your body gives you a much different perspective of your body-target relationship. Different, that is, from the perspective when the ball is positioned off the left side of your chest or even off your left armpit (for the driver). Here's what that change in perspective is all about: With the ball in the center of

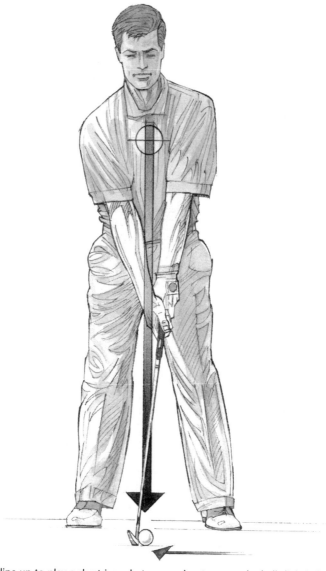

As you line up to play a short-iron shot, remember to move the ball slightly farther back in your stance, with your hands well ahead, and use your chest as a reference point for ball position.

For longer shots, the ball is moved forward in the stance, with your hands slightly ahead or even with the ball.

your body, there is an inclination to aim your body and the club to the right of your target. The reason for this is that when your body is properly aligned with the ball in the middle of your stance, it feels like you're aimed *left* of the target, so you "compensate" by aiming your body to the right of the target. The question follows, of course: Why do you feel like you're aiming left and so, in turn, end up aiming right?

Before you start to work through your pile of 100 balls, make sure you get good and loose. Do your stretching routine (You do have one, don't you? If the answer is "No," we'll help you out later in the chapter) and hit some balls that aren't among your 100. Just a few little flip wedges and then a few full swings so you're nice and limber. You want to strike your 100 balls with full-blooded swings, loose-as-a-goose, midround type swings.

Okay, now you're set. The reason you're going to hit 20 balls with each club is that you're looking for an average. You don't hit every shot in a round squarely—not even a pro does—so you want to come to a conclusion concerning your *average* carry distance with each of these clubs. If you hit one a little thin or a little heavy, don't discount it. Have your helper mark it down. If you hit a super-chunker that goes only 20 yards, or you blade a wedge that flies 120 yards, take those out of the equation. Work out some sort of hand signal, like a thumbs down, that you can use to indicate to your partner not to record those. Once you start to hit the 20 balls with the sand wedge, take your time. Before each one, pick a target (it will help your pal if you aim at your distance markers) and go through your pre-shot checklist. After you hit the shot, relax for a second and give your helper a chance to record the distance.

Once you finish up with the sand wedge, move to the pitching wedge. Give your partner a wave or a yell to indicate you're

The reason is that because you're fairly close to the target, you feel like your body should be aimed *directly at the target*. But your body is never aimed directly at the target, it's aimed along a line parallel to the target. The tendency among high-handicappers is to point the left shoulder directly at the target or to the right of it, which will create problems for you, even when you aim the rest of your body correctly.

switching clubs. If you want to take a breather, go ahead. Remember, you're hitting 100 full shots. That's more than twice the number you hit in a round of golf. Work your way through the 100 balls, 20 per club. If you can't keep track, have your helper let you know when you've hit 20. (Just make sure he or she counts even the ones you might not be putting toward the average—those one or two you hit very poorly.)

When all is said and done, buy your helper a beer (or an ice cream if it's your kid) and sit down and figure out the averages. Make sure you divide by the number of "keepers" you hit. In other words, if you super-chunked one ball with your sand wedge, then you should divide the total distance of the sand wedge shots by 19 instead of 20. You probably knew that, but, what the heck, we're not all calculus majors.

What you should come up with is the average distance you hit each of your short irons under perfect conditions. It's rare that you hit any shot under perfect conditions, but you need to know this information as a baseline factor in choosing a club when you're actually playing. It's also important that you know the average distance you hit a shot, because you never want to make a club choice based on the idea that you're going to hit it perfectly. A misconception most players have is that you hit the ball in 10-yard increments with each club. That's an assumption a lot of golfers make, and it's a bad one. Think about it: Most players figure out a club by starting with some baseline thought such as, "Well, I hit my 7-iron 150 yards, and I've got 140 yards to the target. That must be an 8-iron." Well, maybe you hit the ball in only 8-yard increments from club to club. Which, in this example, means it might still be an 8-iron. But what if you had 120 yards to the hole and you thought, Well, 7-iron equals 150 yards, so 120 yards must equal pitching wedge." If you actually hit the ball in 8-yard increments, you'd be a whole club off in your math. Not good. That's why you need to know the average distance you hit each of your short irons.

The Real Deal

As we noted previously, you rarely hit a shot under perfect conditions. In other words, you hardly ever have a shot that is the perfect distance for a club, a flat lie in short grass, and no wind or other factors such as pressure (be it real or imagined). That's why we call this part of the chapter "The Real Deal," because we're going to talk about how to choose a target on the green and know which club to play to get you there.

The first thing to consider when hitting an approach to a green is the green itself—the danger spots and how to choose your target. You should always start your analysis of a green from the center of the green. The center of the green is the one spot that won't get you into too much trouble, and it works as a good baseline for trying to figure out just how close to the hole you can get. What follows are the items you should weigh in thinking about getting the ball as close to the hole as you can without getting stupid.

Using the middle of the green as your reference point, take a look at where the hole is cut and divide the green around it into zones which you can label the Red, Yellow, and Green Zone.

The Red Zone

You should consider any zone that offers a maximum of one "bailout" area a Red Zone. (By "bailout" area we mean a spot where if you don't hit the shot solidly the ball will still end up safe.) An example of a Red Zone target would be where the hole is cut in the back right portion of the green with a bunker in front and trouble over the green. If there's no trouble on the back left in this example, then you have the back left as a bailout area if you decide to attack the hole. Which, by the way, you're not going to do unless you've got a pitching wedge or a sand wedge in your hand. (Or your gin fizz at the turn was made with a strong hand.) If there's only one safety area other than in the hole, you're looking at a Red Zone target. If you have a distance that requires anything other than a wedge, play for the middle of the green. If you want to attack with the wedge, go ahead, but aim left of the hole and hope it drifts in a little bit. That way if you yank it a bit, you're still safe. If you luck out and push it, you might have a leaner. If you chunk it, you're still okay.

> *It sometimes makes sense to play aggressively, but it always makes sense to play smart.*
>
> *— Jim Flick*

The Yellow Zone

You can qualify any pin placement that offers two bailout areas as a Yellow Zone. You want to check whether the hole is on the side that favors your dominant shot pattern. If you generally fade the ball, that means the hole favors you when it is cut on the right side of the green. If you generally draw the ball, a pin position on the left side of the green works to your favor. If the hole is *not* on the side of the green that favors your shot pat-

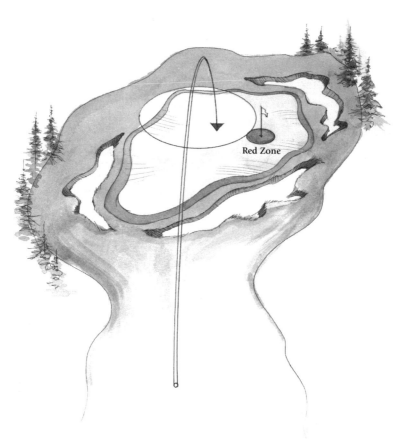

Looking at this flag should make you see red, as in red light. The safe—and smart—play is to aim for the center of the green.

tern, this is not an attack situation. If the hole is on the side of the green that favors your usual ball flight, then you're in an attack situation with any one of your short irons.

The Green Zone

Any time the hole has more than two bailout areas around it, you should be in attack mode. This is the time to go for the pin.

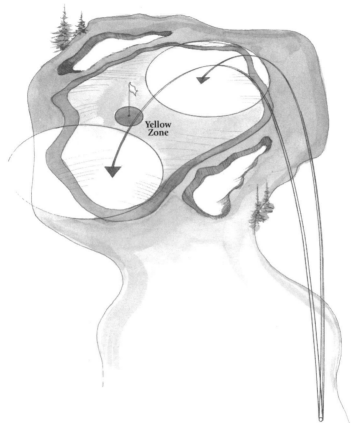

This flag is somewhat accessible, though you should use caution. There are more inviting areas on the green that you can easily hit.

Playing the Shots

Once you determine what sort of zone the hole is situated in, you can start to plan the shot. There is a whole list of things to think about as you prepare to play the shot, and you need to do it quickly. So sit up in that chair and pay attention!

First, you want to start any shot you play with the 7-, 8-, or 9-iron at the center of the green. The reason for this is that

This is a green light special. Fire right at the flag, because a miss in any direction will still put you on the green in easy two-putt range.

while these clubs have a lot of loft on them, they'll still drift a little bit in the direction of your prevailing shot. If you fade the ball and the hole is on the left side of the green, you should always aim at the center of the green. If you hit it straight you'll be fine, and if you hit a fade you'll still catch the right side of the green. However, if you aim right at the flag and hit even a slight pull, you're going to miss the green. Keep in mind that in order to dance you first have to get on the dance floor.

The same logic applies if the pin is on the right and you draw the ball: Always aim at the center of the green with the 7-, 8-, and 9-irons. If you gun for a pin on the right and push the ball, you're off the green. If you aim at the center and accidentally hit that push, you'll be all over the flag! Another consideration is that you never want to "short side" yourself. That means that you never want to miss the green on the same side as the flag. The reason? You'll have one of the toughest up-and-downs in the game because you won't have much room to land your chip or pitch in front of the hole. That means a lot of added pressure, which ups the chances you'll fluff your pitch or chip, or hit it way past the hole into three-putt territory.

With the wedges, follow the zone bailout rules we mentioned earlier.

If the hole is cut in the front of the green, select a club that will put you pin high if you hit it *thin*. Got that? That means *do not* hit the club that will put you pin high if you hit it your average distance. Take the club that will put you pin high if you slightly mis-hit it. The logic behind that? If you hit it thin you're pin high. If you hit it normally, you'll be a few yards past the hole. If you hit it flush you'll be on the middle of the green.

If the hole is cut in the back of the green, you want to choose a club so that if you hit *pure—absolutely flush—*you will put your ball pin high. You don't want to take the club that will put an average hit pin high, because if you hit it flush you'll be over the green. If you make your club selection using this logic, more often than not you'll be a few yards below the hole, which is not a bad spot at all. If you hit it a little thin, you'll be in the middle of the green, no harm no foul.

Any time you have to carry a hazard, give yourself a margin of error. Around the green this usually means bunkers or

Altering the Shape of Your Shot

We mentioned that when you're between clubs the best strategy is to take the longer club, choke down a bit and open up your stance. "Opening" your stance is the easiest way to curve the ball in a controlled manner, and the fade curve helps shorten up the distance of your intentional "overclubbing." There is an important overlooked or misunderstood detail to "opening" your stance that we'd like to point out: Almost any reference you can find to "opening your stance" says something like: "Aim the clubface at the target and aim your body left

water. If water fronts the green, always play at least to the center of the green, even if the hole is cut in the front. Same goes for any bunker fronting the green. In these situations, longer is safer. If in the odd situation the trouble is behind the green, it only follows that the safest route is to play to the front middle of the green and trust your putter. (If you're playing to a green completely surrounded by hazards, you have only one choice for where to land your ball: dead middle of the green.)

Measured Distance vs. Playing Distance

If you're going to be as frighteningly accurate with your short irons as we'd like you to be, you need to have a lot of "street smarts" about club selection. Every shot you play has a measurable distance you can assign to it, especially in short-iron territory. Courses usually have distance markers in the fairway or along the side of the fairway. These distances are measured either to the front edge of the green or the middle of the green. Typically, course yardages are measured to the middle of the green, but you should always check with the pro or the starter of the target." Well, here's a newsflash for you, bub. Your body is aimed left of the target on practically every swing you make. So when you want to "open" your stance, what you want to do is *aim your body to the left of a line running parallel to the target line.* In other words, your feet, hips and shoulders are not parallel to the target line, nor are they simply aimed left of the target line. The key to hitting the type of knockdown shot we described is holding true to what you set up to do: Keep that clubface aimed at the target and swing the club along the line you've set your body on.

before you begin a round (especially if you've never played the course before).

Figuring out the measured distance to the hole is fairly simple from these yardage markers. First you figure the distance from your ball to the yardage marker by pacing off the yards. If your ball is behind the marker, you add the number of paces to the distance. If your ball is ahead of the marker, you subtract the number of paces from the distance. Then you have to figure out that distance in relation to the hole position. A typical green is about 30 yards deep. As you stand out there in the fairway noodling over what club to use, the distance could be as much as 10 yards more than you've paced off, or as much as 10 yards less. The scenarios work like this, assuming the course yardages are to the center of the green: If the hole is in the center of the green, then once you've done your pacing off, you've got the measured distance to the hole. If the hole is in the back of the green, add 10 yards to the distance you've paced off. If the hole is in the front of the green, subtract 10 yards from the distance you paced off. What we just described is how to determine the measured distance from your ball to the hole. This can vary from green to green, but it's an excellent general procedure to follow. If you know a course very well, or the course provides pin placement sheets at the start of your round, you can narrow down the measured distance even more precisely. But the plus- or minus-10 rule works pretty well.

You know as well as we do that golf is not a game of perfect circumstances. You almost never face a situation where the measured distance matches up perfectly with the *playing distance* and with a club in your bag. Knowing that you should calculate playing distance is one of the things that separates the men from the boys in golf—the slashers from the guys who win the bets. One way of defining playing distance is to think of it in terms of *actual* distance or *reality* distance. Allow us a analogy: Let's say you live in Smithville and you want to drive to Ottsville. As the crow flies, it's three miles exactly from your driveway to the town line in Ottsville. However, the roads are rather hilly and curvy between Smithville and Ottsville, so you cannot drive in a straight line. In fact, all those curves in the road add distance to your trip. Let's say in this case that they add a mile of driving. So even though the straight line measurement from Smithville to Ottsville is three miles, you actually have to drive your vehicle four miles to make the trip. That's the difference between measured distance and actual distance (playing distance). Those curves in the road represent the many variables that will affect your ball once it's in flight. Those variables are considerable in golf and represent the difference between landing your ball right on target and somewhere well off target.

These are the variables you should consider in determining the playing distance of a shot:

Any time you're playing a shot into the wind, make a guess at how hard the wind is blowing in terms of miles per hour (mph). For every mph of wind you should add 1 yard to the measured distance to come up with your playing distance.

Downwind, you should subtract a yard from the measured distance for every mph of wind. This is guesswork, of course, but thinking in big numbers will help you tremendously. You might not know the difference between a 2-mph wind and a 4-mph wind, but you should be able to guess the difference between a 5-mph wind and a 10-mph wind. From there, you can guess without hurting yourself much. Where this really comes into play is on very windy days. Trust us, you'll know the difference between 10 mph of wind and 20 mph of wind.

When you're playing into the wind, the ball also curves more, which means it's going to fly even shorter than you figured with the mph calculations. What this means is that if you have a consistent fade or draw, it's going to curve even more and fly shorter.

Downwind the ball is going to fly straighter and farther. The wind neutralizes the sidespin and the backspin. That means that when the ball hits the ground, it's not going to hold. How far it runs depends on the club you're playing. The less loft on the club, the more the ball is going to run. This no-spin/run-when-it-lands effect is seen most strongly in winds of 10 mph or more.

When the green is above you, try to figure out how high above you it is. If it looks about 20 feet higher than you, then add about 7 yards to arrive at your playing distance. If the green is below you, subtract the amount it's below you from the measured distance to arrive at the playing distance. The really tricky part here is not just to notice obviously raised or lowered greens. Check the slope of the entire hole. It could very well be playing uphill for the final 200 yards or for the length of the entire hole. Or it could be downhill all the way. The reason we point this out is that unless you notice this gradual slope, you might not get the true severity of it once you're at your ball. The trick is to guess at the total amount of the slope to the green, then try to figure out how far along the slope you are. If, for example, it looks like the last 200 yards of the fairway run uphill to the green, try to figure out how far along you are in that 200 yards. If the upslope from the 200-yard mark is about 50 feet, and you're about 100 yards out, you've got about 25 feet of slope to factor in. That means you should add about 8 yards to the measured distance to get your actual distance.

If the wind is blowing from right to left, it will obviously straighten out a fade. What you might not know is that it will decrease the carry of the shot. If you hit a draw with a right-to-left wind, the ball will carry farther, and it will also curve more. In both cases, how much distance is added or subtracted and how much curve is added or reduced depends on how strongly the wind is blowing.

In a left-to-right wind, a fade will curve more and carry farther. In the same type of wind, a draw will curve less than normal and carry less than normal. How much the curve and distance is affected is the same as above: It depends on the strength of the wind.

If you're playing the shot from an uphill lie, that is, your left foot is higher than your right foot, then the ball will fly higher and shorter than usual regardless of the wind. And remember on a windy day, that the higher it flies the more the wind will affect it. Downwind the ball will fly farther, so the uphill lie and the wind *may* cancel each other out, depending on the severity of the slope your ball is on and the strength of the wind. If you're playing from a downhill lie—your right foot is higher than your left foot—the ball will fly lower and carry less than normal, but it will run like hell when it hits the ground.

It should be clear to you that on any given shot you could end up with any combination of factors that affect the playing distance of a shot. You have to consider them all and weigh them against each other. Sometimes they cancel each other out, sometimes they all add up.

Matching the Club to the Playing Distance

Once you've gone to all the trouble of figuring out the playing distance of the shot, you are frequently faced with yet another of the reasons that golf is a maddening game. It's called being "between clubs."

Let's say the measured distance of the shot is 125 yards and you determine the playing distance of the shot is 136 yards to the spot on the green where you want to land your ball. That's not what you would call a perfect distance for you because you don't have a club that you hit 136 yards. You typically hit an 8-iron 140 yards and a 9-iron 130 yards. The playing distance you've figured is almost right in the middle of the two clubs—you're between clubs. Here's how you handle those situations when you're between clubs.

Always take the longer of the two clubs. In the above example, you should take the 8-iron.

Slide your hands down on the grip about half an inch. For every inch you choke down on the club, you lose about 10 yards. So if you choke down about half an inch, you'll cut back about 5 yards.

Play the ball slightly back in your stance. With a short iron you typically have the ball positioned at the middle of your torso. Move the ball about an inch to the right (toward your rear foot).

Open your stance slightly in relation to your target. "Opening" your stance means aiming your feet, hips, and shoulders slightly left of the target line. The key here is to leave the clubface aligned at your target, while aiming your body left of the target line. (Read the sidebar on page 56 to make sure you

> *The inexperienced player is always more likely to choose a club because of the number on it rather than because of what he can do with it.*
>
> *— Bobby Jones*

Stretching Your Limits

In the part of this chapter containing the description about how to figure out how far you hit each of your short irons, we mentioned that before you begin that practice session you should first do your stretching routine. By spending just five minutes doing the following six stretches before you begin a round, you'll be able to gain an edge on your buddies and consistently save a few strokes on those opening holes. A nice side benefit of this routine is that it will help protect you from injuries, too. Just one caveat before starting this routine: spend about five minutes walking before you start doing it. This will help raise your body temperature and avoid some of the damage that can result from stretching cold muscles.

Neck rotation: Turn your head to the right, looking as far over your shoulder as possible. Take your left hand and gently push against the left side of your face. Hold for 10 to 15 seconds, then switch sides. *What it does:* Simulates the actual neck movement in a correct swing: left shoulder to chin in your backswing, and right shoulder to chin in your follow-through.

Shoulder stretch: Reach across your body and grasp the back of your right elbow with your left hand. Pull that arm across your body and under your chin as far as you can and hold. Repeat with other arm. *What it does:* Increases the flexibility in the back of the shoulders. Your left shoulder stretches across your chest during the backswing; your right shoulder stretches as you rotate through the shot. Stretching each shoulder will improve your distance.

fully understand the notion of how your body alignment affects the shot.) When you do all these things, you've set yourself up to hit what really good players call a "knockdown shot." So guess what, now you're a really good player! This shot is going

Chest stretch: Clasp your hands behind your back and raise your arms up and out. Inhale to increase the stretch. *What it does:* Stretches your chest and the front of your shoulders, which improves your overall range of motion.

Forward bend: Gently bend forward at the waist until you're able to grasp your ankles, bending your knees as necessary. Let your neck and arms relax as you bend forward slowly from the hips. Holding your ankles, straighten your knees until you feel a comfortable stretch in the backs of your legs. Hold 10 to 15 seconds, then slowly stand, bending your knees as you straighten your trunk. *What it does:* Stretches the lower back, every golfer's most injury-prone area, plus the gluteal muscles and the hamstrings.

Trunk rotation: Standing with your back to a tree or a golf cart, rotate your body to the right so you can grab hold of the tree or cart with both hands without moving your feet. Look over your left shoulder as you stretch. Increase the tension by pulling yourself around a little farther with your hand. Hold for 10 or 15 seconds, then repeat to the other side. *What it does:* Simulates the swing by working the sides of the abdomen and the trunk-rotator muscles.

Side bend: Stand with your feet shoulder-width apart and raise your right arm above your head. While keeping your knees slightly flexed, lean to your left and move your left hand down the outside of your thigh to just above your knee. You should feel a comfortable stretch along the right side of your trunk. Hold for 10 to 15 seconds, then repeat on the other side. *What it does:* Reduces the risk of muscle strain in your rib cage and trunk.

to drift a little left on you unless there is a really strong wind, but you've already accounted for that by aiming your body left of the target line and leaving the clubface aimed at the target. The ball usually ends up where the clubface is aimed.

Final Pre-Swing Moves

You should take a practice swing before every shot you play, but the practice swings you take once the ball is in play differ from those you take when you're on the tee. When you're on the tee you have a flat stance, the ball is teed up, and you're making a very "flat" swing. Those three things make it very, very unlikely that a player of your caliber is going to slam the club into the ground attempting to strike the ball. It's an altogether different story when your ball is sitting out in the fairway and you have a short iron in your hand. First, it's quite possible you won't have a flat lie. Second, your swing is much different with a short iron than it is with your longer clubs. These differences in circumstance mean you have to refocus your practice swing a little bit for your short-iron approaches. Here's what to do.

The first step is the same as what you would do on the tee: Always, always, always swing in the direction of the target. Take your practice swing standing on the same lie you'll have when you play the shot for real. If it's an uphill lie, take an uphill practice swing. If it's a sidehill lie, with the ball above or below your feet, take your practice swing from a similar lie.

Since you don't swing a 9-iron quite as hard at as you do a driver, don't take a practice swing as you would before trying to hit a 250-yard drive. With your short irons, swing at the same speed you'll swing the club when playing the shot.

If you normally take a divot with your short irons, take one with your practice swing. If you normally take a divot and you take a practice swing with the club above the ground through the "impact zone," you're actually rehearsing to top the ball or hit it thin. You don't want to do that, now do you?

4

THE WAY
FROM HERE
TO THERE

We know what you're thinking: This is backwards! Why are these guys telling me about how to hit my short irons before they tell me how to get into position to hit them? The answer is that we wanted to first give you something that would have an impact on your game immediately. And we already gave you the strategy for playing the holes in chapter two. The second reason is that, if you're good enough to break 90, we know you're capable of hitting shots longer than 160 or 170 yards, and occasionally you're going to want to do so. That's fine with us, as long as you play smart long shots. There's a little more to it than just pulling out your 5-iron and blasting the ball in the green's direction. That's what this chapter is about. Your drive sets the table, your short irons get you close. This chapter is going to tell you how not to screw it up in between those two shots.

THE TEE SHOT GONE BAD

On the first pages of this book we told you one of the rules you had to follow to break 90 was to avoid making a big number on any hole, and not to let one bad shot cost you two. The single biggest way this happens is the attempted "hero" shot after a poor drive. We can give you the best possible advice for hitting accurate tee shots, and the truth is that by simply reducing the number of times you hit driver in a round you *will* hit a lot more good tee shots. We've also told you that the short irons are the easiest clubs to hit straight, and they are, but who among us hasn't missed a green with a pitching wedge in our hands? No matter how much we tell you about how to play good tee shots, the truth is you're going to hit a stinker or three from the tee in every round you play. The key is not to let these poor tee shots ruin the entire hole.

If you are in the woods, don't act like a seamstress. Your job is not to thread needles but to get the ball back into the fairway.

— Arnold Palmer

The biggest temptations after a poor tee shot are usually to try to thread the ball through a gap in the trees or to try an unrealistic shot from a poor lie. The first rule of hitting a tee shot into the trees is to get out of the trees on the next shot. And the easiest way to safety is the path of least resistance. That means unless you're on the last hole of the club championship match and your opponent is sitting two inches from the hole for birdie, you should never, ever try to thread the ball through the three-inch gap in the trees just because that's the direct path toward the green. The path of least resistance from the trees is the path with the fewest trees blocking your way to the fairway. Forget about where the green is. If the path of least resistance means you have to play backward to get to the fairway, do it. Don't even think twice about it.

Since a typical recovery shot from the trees needs to travel only 20 or 30 yards, you're almost always best off playing a low shot. So club selection is important: You want a club that will get the ball in the air for 15 yards or so, and then run the rest of the way. You don't want to play your wedges on recovery shots from the trees, since getting the ball up in the air is just going to put it up where the branches hang from the trees. Every situation is different, but for the most part your best bet is to take a 7-iron or 8-iron and hit a little punch shot through a wide-open gap back to the fairway.

These punch shots require you to concentrate—they aren't throw-away shots and the strokes count just as much as any other shot. The first thing you should do after identifying the safest route to the fairway is to check your lie. The things you want to check for are loose impediments around the ball, roots and imbedded rocks around the ball, and any loose impediments underneath the ball such as leaves or pine needles. Clear away all the loose impediments around the ball without moving the ball. Don't move anything that is actually touching the ball, because you may cause the ball to move, and that's a penalty. Second, look for any protruding roots or rocks in the ground around the ball—we'd like you to get safely back to the fairway, but we don't want you breaking your wrist in the process. If there's anything like a root or rock in the area around the ball and you think you're going to hit it with the club through impact, take a drop. It's not worth a trip to the hospital, and you ain't Sergio Garcia.

If the ball is sitting on top of pine needles or leaves, it's easy to fluff this shot. To avoid this, take these steps: Play the ball in the middle of your stance, off the middle of your chest. Open up your stance ever so slightly. Choke down on the club about an inch. Do not ground the club at address, because you'll probably cause the ball to move if you do so. When you make your punch swing, hold on a little more tightly with your left hand, and at impact keep your right wrist cupped—don't turn it over as you do on a full swing.

The other big drive killer is a poor lie that leaves you unable to effectively advance the ball toward the target. These sorts of lies would include grass deep enough so that the ball is at least a half inch below the tops of the blades of grass; a ball lying in an old divot in the rough or any other depression in the rough; a ball up against a tree; a ball lying on any sort of severe side-hill lie, that is, the ball is above your feet or below your feet enough that you feel very uncomfortable addressing the ball.

When the ball is lying in deep rough or in an old divot in the rough, the best play is to take a sand wedge or pitching wedge, play the ball back in your stance, and just hack it out onto the fairway. Deep rough is a killer—if you try to ignore it you're going to end up moving the ball just a few inches. Same thing goes for old divots or any hole in the ground in the rough. It's bad enough you have to contend with the long grass. Trying to force the clubhead through the grass and then down extra far into the divot to muscle out with a middle iron just isn't going to work, Hercules.

If the ball is up against a tree, you've got two things to worry about: How close it is to the base of the tree, and how the lowest hanging branches are going to affect your swing. If you don't have at least a ball's width of distance between your ball and the base of the tree, take a drop or you run the risk of killing yourself. And we can assure you that if you do that, you'll never break 90. If there are branches impeding your backswing at any point before you get the club waist high, take a drop. If you don't, you run the risk of forcing an awkward mini-swing that could result in a whiff, near-whiff, or the ball moving only a few inches. And you still won't be clear of the problems you had in the first place. If you have a clear back-swing and there are branches hanging down in front of the ball, you have to determine if there's enough room for the ball to scoot under if you punch a long iron. If it's iffy, take a drop. If you don't, you could end up with the ball under the tree on your next shot.

Of course, when we talk about "taking a drop" we mean declaring your ball unplayable and taking a single penalty stroke. In almost every case, you can get yourself free and clear of the trouble for that single stroke. You can declare a ball unplayable anywhere on the course except in a water hazard. In many cases it's the smart thing to do.

If you're playing a course that has severe mounding off to the sides of the fairways, and on that mounding there is some significant rough, you need to be very careful with any lie where the ball is above or below your feet. Our recommendation: Since the fairway is flat and

There is such a thing as an unplayable lie. And there is such a thing as an unplayable shot. It's a smart golfer who recognizes both.

— Tony Lema

the place you're at isn't, play back to the fairway. The easiest way to do this is to angle your body with the hill and play on a straight line back to the fairway. Choke up on the club, play the ball well back in your stance, and get back to playing the hole in a sensible manner. (The reason you don't want to try to advance these shots toward the green: If you're off to the left side of the fairway with the ball below your feet, the ball is going to squirt to the right on you at a wicked angle, and you won't be able to control where it goes. If you're off to the right side of the fairway, there's a good chance the grass and the swing plane you're forced into will smother the club and the ball through impact and leave you with the same predicament.)

There are two final types of When Good Drives Turn Bad. The first is when the ball ends up in a fairway bunker. When this happens, you can remember your considerations with the Three Ls: lie, lip and length. Your number one goal is to get out of the bunker, and the lie has the most say in that matter. If the ball is buried, it's a no-brainer. Take your sand wedge and blast out to the fairway. If you have a good lie, that is, you can put the clubface directly onto the back of the ball, then you need to size up the lip and determine the amount of loft you'll need to clear the lip. You should always give yourself a one-club cushion here. If you think a 6-iron will clear the lip, go with a 7-iron. You're going to be playing the ball back in your stance and that's going to reduce the effective loft of the club you choose. If the lie and the lip tell you that you can have a go at the green, you should try it only if you can hit a 7-wood, 9-wood, 11-wood, or 6-iron through sand wedge. If you can't hit those, don't try for the green. If you have a good lie but the lip dictates that you can't reach the green, you should use the following rule (as you should for any layup shot): Take a club that if hit well will leave you short of the next batch of trouble.

These are the basics for playing a fairway bunker shot:

- Dig in with your feet and get a good solid stance.
- Play the ball slightly right of center in relation to your body. You want to make sure you hit the ball before the sand, and this ball position will help you do that.
- Open your stance to the left of the target, but keep the clubface square to the target. The ball will fade a little bit if you hit it correctly.
- Choke up about half an inch on the club. This is one thing many players forget to do, because they fail to realize that

they've lowered themselves when they dig into the sand. In other words, you've "raised" the ground up toward you, so you have to shorten the club.

- Keep your lower body quiet during your swing. Make the swing mostly with your shoulders and arms. Whatever you do, don't overswing.
- Follow through.

And that's it. You're out of the fairway bunker.

The final type of bad drive is the worst kind: a ball out of bounds. When this happens, all we can say is: Take a deep breath, take a club with more loft, take your time, and play to the side of the hole away from the O.B.

THE PATH TO RIGHTEOUSNESS

This chapter is about setting yourself up to play those wicked short irons we told you about in the last chapter. It's about choosing the right path. (Give us an "Amen!" there, brother.) Yes, the right path will set you free to go crazy with those short irons.

The correct path to the green is the one with the fewest obstacles between you and the green. It should also offer a good angle toward the green for the subsequent shot. If you don't have both of these things in hand, then you need to rethink the shot you have in mind.

When we talk about the "right" angle to the green, we're talking about giving yourself a chance to play toward the widest part of the green. In this sense, we're talking about the "wide" part of the green being the part with the most room between the edge of the green and the hole. When you play to this wide part, you give yourself the best chance of getting up and down if you miss the green. (If you have a green light situation and a wedge,

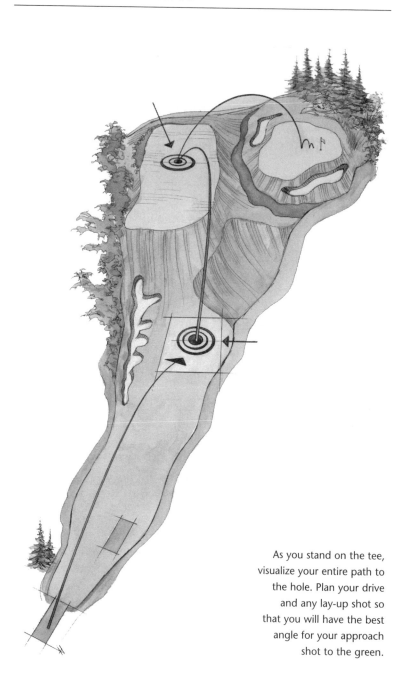

As you stand on the tee, visualize your entire path to the hole. Plan your drive and any lay-up shot so that you will have the best angle for your approach shot to the green.

you can still fire at the flag. We're assuming here that you're going to use all those guidelines we gave you previously.)

In case you're not clear about it, in this little section we're talking about hitting what are commonly referred to as "layup" shots. Trust us on this, they *are not* the easiest shots in the game, and they require your full concentration. The quickest way to add strokes to your score is to just grab a club and whack it in the general direction of the green. We can't emphasize this point enough: When you decide to play a positional layup shot, you have to bear down on it as much as any other shot you play.

The first thing you have to do is pick the spot you want as your target. That spot should have three characteristics: It should offer you an angle playing "in" toward the wide part of the green as defined above; it should offer you a fairly flat lie (and of course should be in the fairway); finally, it should leave you at a distance where you can swing fully with one of your short irons. You should never put yourself between clubs just because you weren't thinking about it. We realize it's inevitable you're going to end up between clubs, but if you can avoid it by properly planning your layup shot, you should do so.

These types of shots are called layup shots because you are laying up not only short of the green but short of any trouble as well. This has an impact on your club selection for the layup shot. First, you want to make sure you're well short of any trouble you cannot easily carry. We'd say well short means at *least* 20 yards. (And make sure you factor in the wind, your lie, and the slope of the ground!) Second, when playing your layup shot, you should select a club you can hit for the full measure. Please don't try to hit a little half shot with your 3-wood. Hit a full-blooded 5-iron instead, or whatever club may get you to your target spot. You want to make a full swing on these shots because you'll reduce the likelihood of the poor swings that players routinely make when just "slapping something up around the green."

The last step before playing a layup shot is to go through your full preshot routine. No matter how "intermediate" the shot seems to you, it can still get you into trouble. The best way to give it the importance it deserves is to go through your full routine prior to making your swing. That includes making a good practice swing. If we had a dollar for every time we've seen a player walk up to a layup shot and just slap it without taking a practice swing, we could buy Greg Norman's airplane.

Lester, You Are Clear for Approach

There are two kinds of position shots—the kind you hope ends up on the green, and the kind you hope to put in position so that you can play the next shot to the green. If you're serious about breaking 90 and you're buying what we're selling in this book, you'll be hitting more of the latter type. However, we realize you can easily reach a lot of holes out there in two shots if you hit a good drive, and we know you're going to try to do that. So if you've got anything more than a 5-iron in your hand and you're playing toward the green, we'd like you to consider the following advice.

The first thing to think about is club selection. We're not big fans of long irons, but we realize that almost every player carries at least a 4-iron. You might even fancy the 3-iron for all we know. Whatever. We suggest a green light for long irons when the situation has all of the following attributes:

- There is no trouble in front of the green that is going to prevent the ball from running onto the green if you mis-hit it.
- You're playing into the wind.
- The hole is cut in the back of the green.

- The green is at least average in depth, preferably even deeper than normal.

Hmmm. Notice anything about all of those suggestions? They make an assumption, don't they? And that assumption is that there is a hell of a chance that you're going to hit the ball thin. That's the most common mistake with long irons. But if you play them only when the shot has all of the above characteristics, you'll be fine. If you hit it well, you're in business. If you hit it badly, you're still in business. We also suggest you aim for the side of the green that will offer you the most room between you and the hole in case you miss the green to that side. In other words, if the hole is on the left, aim for the right side of the green, and if the hole is on the right, aim for the left side of the green. If you mis-hit the ball, you'll probably miss the green on the side you aimed at, and you'll be facing an easier up-and-down situation.

If it's a toss-up between a long iron and a fairway wood, you should always reach for the fairway wood if:

- The green is elevated, that is, it's higher than the fairway.
- There is a bunker or other hazard directly fronting the green, or close enough that it presents only a narrow gap that a ball would have to get lucky to run through.
- You're downwind or there's virtually no wind.
- You need the ball to stop almost immediately when it hits the green.

You can tell that we firmly believe you'll have an easier time hitting the fairway woods than you will the long irons. Truly, there is little argument in favor of the long irons because they are the best choice in only a handful of situations. The fairway woods fly higher (always a good thing except dead into strong winds) because of the weight of the sole of the club; they fly longer due to the length of the shaft; they fly straighter (they have more loft); and they give you more room for error than long irons (hit the thing anywhere on the clubface and the ball will fly okay).

We'll cover the basics of the fairway wood swing and ball position later in the book, but for now concentrate on two things when you're making a pass at your fairway woods. First, don't play the ball all the way up off your left shoulder as you do with your driver. Move the ball back slightly in your stance—about halfway between your shoulder and the center of your body. If you err in any direction, err toward the center of your body. Second, make sure you make a controlled swing. Think about your tempo when you're swinging. You don't need to hammer on your fairway woods. They're among the easiest clubs in your bag to hit. Let the club do the work. Another way to think of this is to swing in balance—shift your weight back and through evenly without throwing your body all over the place. You're not tackling someone. You're just hitting that itty-bitty ball.

5

THE WORLD'S GREATEST SHORT GAME

Consistently low scoring is an art form that involves much more than just proper technique. When you hear good players talk about the ability to "score" what they mean is that a player knows how to make low numbers even when he's not having his best day striking the ball. And the truth of the matter is that there are not many days an average golfer can call his best ballstriking day. That means to break 90 on a regular basis you have to know how to keep yourself in the game when you're not hitting the ball well. The way you keep yourself in the big game is to have a great little game. This chapter is going to teach you how to have a short game so good that you'll never have a day when you feel you can't break 90.

The first step to improving your short game is to understand the basic shots available to you—the chip shot and pitch shot. Then we'll get into all sorts of interesting concepts like ball spin and flop shots and all that good stuff.

CHIPPING AWAY AT 90

Other than putting, a chip shot is the simplest shot in golf to execute, which is precisely why it is so mysterious that so many players struggle with chipping. Perhaps some of the difficulty arises from a lack of confidence over whether the chip is the proper shot for a given situation. Should I putt this or chip it? Chip it or pitch it? Should I have red or white wine with the fish? These are questions which leave golfers shaking their heads. We're going to take a little guesswork out of the decision-making process for you. Here's how you decide whether to putt, chip, or pitch.

For two weeks devote 90 percent of your practice time to chipping and putting, and only 10 percent to the full swing. If you do this, your 95 will turn into 90. I guarantee it.

— Harvey Penick

You should always putt when your ball is on the green, and whenever you can when your ball is off the green. That may sound like it leaves a lot of room for interpretation, but it's really quite simple and involves only three things to consider: (1) Can you make the ball travel the distance between you and the hole using a normal putting stroke? (2) Can you swing the club back and through without getting it stuck in the grass? (3) Is there a clear path between your ball and the hole? (By clear we mean there are no big tufts of grass or anything else that will significantly slow or stop the progress of the ball.) If the answer is yes to all three of these questions, then you should putt.

If the answer is no to any of the above questions, then you should chip or pitch. You should chip the ball anytime it's too long to putt but you're within 20 yards of the front of the green and there is no rough between your ball and the hole. If there is any rough, you should play a pitch shot. If you're on the collar of the green you would normally putt, but if there's anything on the line of the putt that can't be moved and will throw the ball off line, you should chip.

If your ball is sitting up in the rough and there are fewer than 3 yards of rough between your ball and the fairway-length grass of the collar of the green, you should chip. By "sitting up" we mean that the ball is sitting mostly on top of the grass (as opposed to settled down between the blades of grass) and that you can get the clubface cleanly on the ball without getting the club tangled in the grass.

You should play a pitch shot any time you have to carry 3 or more yards of rough to get the ball to the edge of the green. You should also play some type of pitch shot whenever the bottom half of the ball is down in the rough. If you can see only the top half of the ball, play a pitch shot. Two more pitch shot indicators: From the fairway, you should play a pitch anytime you feel that the shot is too long to comfortably play a chip shot. Finally, when the golf course is exceedingly wet, you want to play pitch shots almost exclusively. It's very difficult to predict how far a ball will run on wet ground.

How to Play a Chip Shot

We've devoted an entire chapter to putting a little later in the book, so for now we're going to focus on the other aspects of your short game. Once you've assessed a situation and determined that you should play a chip shot, the first thing you have to do is decide which club to use to play the shot.

When executing most chip shots, you're attempting to move the ball only a few feet or yards in the air. And for the most part you want to get the ball up in the air briefly and then back down on the ground—it's more projecting the ball forward rather than up in the air. You can use any club to chip. Which club you use is based almost entirely on the distance between your ball and the hole. The farther away the hole, the less loft you want on the club.

A large part of having a good short game is to eliminate distractions and focus on the shot. One way of doing this is to limit the number of clubs from which you choose for a chip shot. If you've struggled with your short game in the past, you might want to consider trying the following. Tell yourself before a round that in any chipping situation you're going to use either a 5-iron, a 7-iron, or a 9-iron. If you're close to the hole, use the 9-iron. If the hole is about halfway between you and the other side of the green, use the 7-iron. If the hole is all the way on the other side of the green, use the 5-iron. Maybe you don't like odd numbers and would rather use your 6-iron, 8-iron, and pitching wedge. It doesn't really matter. The point is that by simplifying club selection you can focus more intently on the other aspects of the shot.

The playing of a basic chip shot can be simple if you're consistent in your setup and stroke. As you'll see later in the putting chapter, one of the keys to good putting is to keep your body and head "quiet" or steady throughout the stroke. Since chipping and putting closely resemble each other, you'd be correct if you guessed that the leading key to consistent chipping is keeping a steady head and body. Here are the other things to focus on when playing a chip shot.

Open Lower Body

Usually when you hear about opening your stance it's a reference to your entire alignment. With a chip shot, that's not the case. This shot uses such a small swing that you couldn't possibly affect the "shape" of the ball flight, which is the normal reason for opening your stance. In this case we simply want to help you feel more comfortable over the ball and make it easier to get the club moving in the manner you want. So here's what we want you to do. We want you to pick a target and set the lead edge of the club square to the target. Then step in and set your body square just like any other shot: shoulders, hips, and feet parallel to the target line. Now, open your feet and hips ever so slightly—aim them a little left of the target line. Keep your shoulders parallel to the target line and the clubface square to the target. (You may remember that earlier we mentioned you can't move your hips without your upper body responding, but that applies only when you're in motion. When your body is still, you can do what we describe here.)

Play Ball Back in Stance
You want to strike every chip shot with a descending blow. This means you want the club moving down, not up, when you strike the ball. When you play a chip shot there is no need to attempt to lift the ball into the air. You want it in the air only for a few seconds, and the club can do all the work here. (To take this point a bit further, there is never a situation in golf where you should try to lift or "help" the ball into the air. Your setup and your club can always get the job done for you.) One of the things you want to be conscious of when playing a chip shot is that the club needs to make contact with the ball before it makes contact with the ground. The easiest way to do this is to move the ball back in your stance. We told you before that you don't want to use your feet as a reference point for ball position since the width of your stance with your feet varies from shot to shot. What we want you to do here is to play the ball to the right of the center of your body—about midway between the center of your chest and your right shoulder. This

will help you make clean contact. This is especially important because you are naturally going to take a more narrow stance with your feet when playing a chip shot.

Place Weight on Left Side

Another thing that helps create a descending blow is having your weight on your left leg. The best way to do this is just to feel like you're leaning slightly toward your target. Anytime you think about weight and its placement, it follows naturally to wonder how much of your weight we're talking about. Obviously, we don't want you leaning so far toward the target that you feel you're going to fall over. When you have your setup correct, you should feel like you have about 60 percent or so of your weight leaning toward the target.

Choke Down on the Club

In baseball they call it choking up on the bat, maybe because the bat is pointing toward the sky and you have to slide your hands up to shorten the bat. We'll refer to it as choking down, since the club is pointed down and what you to do is effectively shorten the club. You want to do this because when you shorten the club you make it easier to control, and these shots are all about control. You should choke down enough to the point that you feel you have your putter in your hands. By doing this you're gaining more control and you're not losing anything, since you're not concerned with generating power with this shot.

Allow Your Arms to Hang Loose

Tension is a shot-killer in golf, and to avoid it we always encourage you to have your arms hanging freely from your shoulders when you set up for any shot. You still want to have your arms loose for this shot, but make sure you have enough space between the butt of the club and your body so that you

The correct set-up and technique for the common chip shot. Three important reminders: (1) at address, weight and hands are ahead; (2) very little body movement during back and through strokes; (3) keep the lead wrist firm through and past impact.

can swing the club without whacking yourself with the portion of the club sticking out above the top of your hands.

Reach Back for the Ball

Since the ball is back in your stance, you'll want to feel you're reaching back for the ball a little bit with your arms. This is different from having your arms hanging straight down as you would to hit a full 9-iron, for instance. You don't want to overdo this, but it's a good sensation to key on because it will help you do two things: (1) straighten your left arm, (2) set your right wrist at the proper angle for executing the shot. As it relates to your left arm, you're going to want to keep it straight throughout your chipping stroke, so it's a good idea to pre-set that position. (Do not confuse "straight" with "stiff." Stiff equals tension and you don't want that.) Same goes for your right wrist. The angle you set it at address is an angle you want to maintain through impact, especially through the ball. When you cock your wrist at address, that angle should be maintained throughout the entire stroke. What exactly is that angle? It's just a slight cocking of the wrist to the right. By maintaining it throughout the stroke, you keep your hands ahead of the clubhead, which is exactly what you want.

Set Eyes Slightly Inside the Target Line

This will happen almost naturally, but since the club is longer you want to make sure you're not hovering over the ball as you do when you putt. That will throw you off balance.

Set Club on Its Toe at Address

We'll give you a quick refresher here, just in case you have equipment amnesia. The heel of the club is the side where the shaft joins the clubhead. The toe of the club is the opposite side

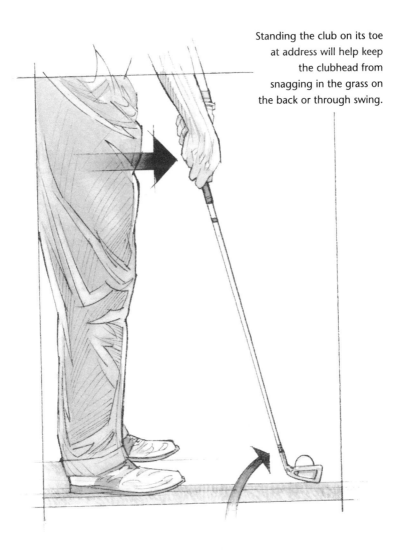

Standing the club on its toe at address will help keep the clubhead from snagging in the grass on the back or through swing.

of the club, or the portion of the clubface farthest away from you when you address the ball. One of the common misfires when chipping the ball is to get the club caught in the grass during the takeaway, or to get it snagged in the grass as the club approaches the ball prior to impact. This happens to even the best of players, so it's a good idea to take measures to avoid it. Our surefire suggestion for avoiding this is to stand the club on its toe at address. Another way of thinking of this is to have the shaft of the club closer to perpendicular with the ground than you normally would. You don't want the shaft to be actually perpendicular, but close to it. By doing this you keep a good portion of the clubhead clear of the grass but leave enough of the clubface in position to contact the ball. There is one more huge benefit to setting the club in this manner: The ball will come off the clubface with a "dead" feel to it every time, which means you don't have to worry about catching the chip too pure and sending it motoring way past your target.

Think About Putting

The commonalities between chipping and putting are plentiful. For starters, you want the ball to travel along the ground toward the hole as much as possible. The chipping stroke itself is quite like the putting stroke, too. Once you've made all the proper adjustments in your setup to play a chip, you simply move your arms and shoulders back and forth, all the while maintaining any angles you've set in your wrist and arms. The proper stroke should feel very natural to you.

Good players often look at the hole when taking their practice putting strokes. By doing this they get a sense of how far to swing the putter back and through. It's a good idea to do this with your chip shots, too. As with putting, another good way to gauge the length of your arm swing is to imagine how far back and through you'd move your throwing arm if you were going to roll the ball toward the hole. You should hit most chip shots about as hard as you would a putt from the same distance. Just remember, once you've gauged the distance, focus on your intermediate target. That is your target point.

THE COMMON MISTAKES OF CHIPPING

Bad results don't happen on their own. When you skull a chip shot that goes running across the green, or stub a shot, it usually happens for one of the following reasons. Knowing them will help you avoid them.

Standing Too Far Away from the Ball

If you get your body too far away from the ball you have to stick your arms out toward the ball. Any time you feel you're extending your arms "out" toward the ball, you're in trouble. This is going to create tension and you don't want that. Tension will block you from feeling the weight of the clubhead, and having a good sense of the clubhead is vital to having good touch on your chip shots. Another reason you don't want to stand too far away from the ball is that the second you move the clubhead it will swing immediately to the inside and off the target line. When you're chipping you want the club to move straight back and through along the target line. When the club moves inside (or outside) the target line, you're going to have trouble making clean contact and keeping the shot on line.

Using a Club with Too Much Loft

A chip shot is a running shot. Everything you do in your setup is designed to push the ball forward at a low trajectory. If you consistently come up short of your target, try using less-lofted clubs.

Opening Your Shoulders in Relation to the Target Line

If you remember, we mentioned opening your feet and hips, but keeping your shoulders square. If you open your shoulders too, you'll probably yank the chip to the left of your target.

Selecting Your Club Using Simple Math

Perhaps you're the type of personality who doesn't like things to be even slightly vague. You like to have things precise in your world— everything right down to the number. If so, you're probably not too crazy about the fact that we didn't give you a surefire recipe for how to choose the exact club to use on any given chip. The reason we didn't give any absolute rules for choosing a club is that we like to leave a little wiggle room for folks who aren't so turned on by iron-clad rules. But, since you're the type who likes formulas for things, here's one for choosing a club for chipping.

For every chip shot, there are two constants and two variables. The two constants are the spot where you're going to land the ball and the number 12. The two variables are where the ball lies and how far the hole is from your landing area. This is slightly tricky, so pay attention.

Step one: Well, step one isn't really a step at all. It's just an acknowledgment of one of your absolutes. The landing area (the place where you want to land your ball on the green, not where you want it to stop) is always one full pace onto the green. One nice big stride— about a yard.

Step two: Pace off the distance from the ball to the landing area. This is the distance the ball will fly in the air. Convert the distance from yards to feet.

Step three: Pace off the distance from the landing area to the hole to determine precisely how far the ball will roll. Convert the distance from yards to feet.

Step four: Combine the two numbers into a fraction. The flight portion of the fraction will always be lower than the roll part of the fraction. You can call your fraction the flight-to-roll ratio (or carry-to-roll ratio). The lower number always goes on top.

Step five: Reduce the fraction to its lowest common form.

Step six: Subtract the denominator (the bottom number in your fraction) from the number 12 (your second constant). What you have left is the number of the iron you should play for your chip shot.

Okay, that might sound fine in theory, but we'll walk you through an example just to make sure you get it.

Remembering that the landing area for your shot is always 1 yard (3 feet) onto the green along the target line, you pace off the distance from the ball to the landing area and decide it's about 7 feet (two and one-third paces).

Next, you pace off the distance from the landing area to the hole and find that it's roughly seven paces, or 21 feet.

Make your fraction: $\frac{7}{21}$.

Reduce the fraction to its lowest common form and you have $\frac{1}{3}$.

Subtract 3 from 12 and you're left with 9. That means you should use your 9-iron. Now just swing your 9-iron as hard as you would your putter for a putt of the same length. If your fraction doesn't work out to give a clean ratio, add or subtract to the denominator until you get to the nearest number (up or down) that will give you a clean fraction you can reduce to a lowest form without anything left over.

Here's a chart that will help make all of this a bit more simple.

CLUB	CARRY	ROLL
SW	1 part	1 part
PW	1 part	2 parts
9-iron	1 part	3 parts
8-iron	1 part	4 parts
7-iron	1 part	5 parts
6-iron	1 part	6 parts
5-iron	1 part	7 parts
4-iron	1 part	8 parts
3-iron	1 part	9 parts

If you have any questions, call MIT collect. Tell them Adams and Tomasi told you to call.

Playing the Ball Too Far Forward in Your Stance

This one is a killer, and also the most common mistake. Getting the ball too far forward in your stance almost guarantees that you're going to catch the ball when the club is swinging up rather than down. And when you hit the ball when the club is swinging up, chances are you're going to catch the middle portion of the ball with the lead edge of the clubface. So if you're consistently blading your chip shots across the green, check your ball position. It's the most likely culprit.

How to Be an Ace Pitcher

There are three main differences between a pitch and a chip—the amount of time the ball is in the air, the height of the ball while it's in the air, and the amount of backspin on the ball. The ball stays in the air longer because of the length of the swing used, flies higher because it is almost always played with a lofted club, and has more backspin on it because of the bigger swing and the angle of the swing. That last bit—the backspin—allows you a fair measure of control over what your pitch shots do once they've hit the ground.

The short answer as to when you should play a pitch shot is whenever you can't chip. Hold it, maybe we should make that "whenever you can't chip effectively." There's a big difference. You can always attempt to chip, but it might not be the right shot for the situation. (We see people do this all the time at our schools.) For example, if your ball is 25 feet off the green and in the rough, and the hole is only seven or eight paces onto the green, does a chip seem in order? Hardly, because the idea behind a chip shot is to get the ball back on the ground after only a few inches or feet of flight. In the situation described, you need a shot with some hang time (to carry the rough) and some height (to land softly and minimize the amount of roll).

That last part—about minimizing the roll of the ball once it hits the ground—is an example of how a pitch shot can be altered to fit the circumstances for any situation. Sometimes you might want the ball to stick like Velcro, another time you might want it to roll just a little bit, maybe a few feet, and still another time you might want it to run halfway across the green. Those are the three options you have when playing a pitch shot. We'll call them (in order) the Biter, the Stroller, and the Sprinter. Let's take a look at each type of shot. First we'll look at the similarities in executing each type of pitch, then the specifics of the pitch itself.

> *In many ways, the pitch shot is the scoring shot in golf. To a master of the pitch, there's no pin that isn't accessible.*
>
> *— Raymond Floyd*

Align the Clubface with the Target

Your target for a pitch is the place you want the ball to land. And, like any other shot, you should determine that while standing behind the ball. Make sure you aim with the lead edge of the clubface (the bottom part of the face) as opposed to the top of the clubface, especially if you have offset clubs.

Butt of the Shaft Always Points to the Center of Your Body

Regardless of which type of shot you play, or where you position the ball in relation to your body, the butt of the handle should point at the center of the body. Keep this in mind, because you'll be changing your ball position for the three types of pitch shots.

Swing Club Along Your Shoulder Lines

You'll be adjusting the position of your body's aiming points for each of the shots. No matter where you aim your body, always swing the club along the line where your shoulders are aimed. Paying too much attention to how your feet are set will diminish your accuracy.

Distance Is Determined by Length of Swing

When you're playing a pitch shot, the key strategic decision is where you're going to land the ball. Subsequently, you'll want to decide how hard to swing to get the ball to that point.

Unfortunately, there's no precise method of measuring your swing against the distance of the shot it produces. However, you can get a feel for this in a fairly simple manner as long as you remember this: When playing a pitch shot, you should always swing the club back and through the same distance. You can practice this on the practice range. Pick a target about 20 yards away and, using your sand wedge, concentrate on getting the ball to land near that target by making swings where the backswing and follow-through are equal in length. If you practice this with some regularity, varying the distance to the target, you'll soon acquire a feel for how far back and through to swing the club to produce shots of various distances.

Height Is Determined by Ball Position

This is important to remember. You may often hear commentators on television mentioning that a player is "laying the clubface wide open." You don't have to lay the clubface wide open to play any shot. By changing the ball position in your stance, you'll alter the effective loft of the club you're using.

Playing the Biter

This is the shot you want to play when you have very little green to "work with," as they say on television. What that means is that there is very little room between the edge of the green and the hole on the side where your ball rests.

Play this shot with a sand wedge or, if you carry one and the distance is appropriate, a lob wedge. The lob wedge is a weird club. If you have one, you should spend some time figuring how far you can hit it with various lengths of swing. We say weird because sometimes it's hard to believe you can make such a long swing and produce such a short shot. Another thing that makes the lob wedge somewhat awkward is that poor players often try to hit it too far. You have to know your maximum comfortable distance with this club—the distance of shot you can play without overswinging—or you're going to produce a lot of frustrating results.

You'll get the maximum loft out of the club by playing the ball forward in your stance. By forward we're talking about just slightly left of the center of your body. Any farther forward than that and you bring the possibility of a skulled shot into play.

Set your body slightly open to the target. This means that your shoulders, hips, knees, and feet should be parallel to a line that runs from your ball to a point slightly left of your target. Remember to keep the clubface aimed directly at your target.

Depending upon the length of the shot you want to produce, make the following adjustments: The longer the shot, the wider your stance and the higher up on the grip you hold the club. The shorter the shot, the more narrow your stance and the more you should choke down on the club.

Swing the club along your shoulder line, making sure to complete the follow-through. When you follow through, here's a checkpoint: The knuckles on your left hand should be facing the sky when you've finished swinging.

PLAYING THE STROLLER

This shot will carry about two-thirds of the way to the hole and roll the rest. Play the ball in the center of your body, directly in the center of your chest. Set your body square to the target, that

Do the Funky Chip-In

One of the most awkward situations you can face is to be off the green and close to the hole, but have the ball sitting directly up against the miniature wall of grass formed where the collar of the green meets the rough. When the ball is sitting right up against this wall of grass, or just a half inch or so into the rough, it can pose a problem. The problem is that you want to get the advantages of putting—better speed control and truer line—but you don't want to get the putter snagged in the grass.

Your options in these situations are limited. You can use your putter and hope you don't get it snagged in the grass, but hope doesn't usually get you too far in golf. You can also try to play a chip shot, but that opens up the possibility of hitting the ball too hard in an attempt to avoid stubbing it.

The solutions for these situations can be seen almost weekly on the PGA Tour. Note we said solutions, because you have two options. The first is the bellied wedge shot, and the second is the metal wood chip. Neither shot has a great name, but both can make your life a lot easier.

The bellied wedge is played using your sand wedge and is the simpler of the two shots. You grip down on the club enough so that the lead edge of the clubface is level with the center of the ball. This means you choke down more than you normally do for a chip shot. In this case, you're probably choked down a good 3 inches on the club. Unlike other chips, you don't want to hit down on this shot, either. If anything, you want to catch it slightly on the upswing or at the precise bottom of the stroke. That's really boiling the shot down a little too precisely, however. All you need to do is set up like you're putting the ball. That means you would have the ball slightly left of center in your stance. You also don't want to set your hands quite as far ahead of the ball as you would for a normal chip. You don't want the big angle in your right wrist. Keep your wrists completely out of the stroke. Just set your weight on your left side at address, and don't ground the club. Keep it above the ground and hovering right around the equator of the ball. You don't do this by standing straighter—you do it by choking down on the club as mentioned earlier. Then it's just a matter of a nice, smooth stroke. Take the club back and through the ball the same distance. Do not pull up short on the follow-through—strike it just like a putt.

The metal wood chip was first widely used by Chi Chi Rodriguez and it's been popularized by Tiger Woods. Chi Chi was the ultimate shotmaker, and this is one you can borrow from him if you're more comfortable with it. This one works better than the bellied wedge when the ball is a few inches off the collar—say about 2 or 3 inches. The club of choice for this shot is a 3-wood, which has enough loft to lift the ball up ever so slightly to clear the rough, and then get it running along the ground like a putt. When we say ever so slightly, we mean ever so slightly—so much so that you can't really see it happen. Like the bellied wedge, this shot is all about the setup. One thing this shot has in common with other chip shots is that you want to get the club up on its toe slightly. You want to have the shaft nearly perpendicular to the ground, which mean you'll have to stand fairly close to the ball. Choke well down on the club—enough so that you get the clubface on the top two-thirds of the ball, but not so much that you get it snagged in the grass. You should open your stance slightly and play the ball back in your stance—right around the center of your body. This open stance will give you room to handle a club that is extremely long to be used in this situation.

What this shot does have in common with the bellied wedge is the lack of wrist action. You just sort of pop the club on the back of the ball with a putting stroke and follow through.

is, parallel to a line that runs from the ball directly to the target. Swing the club straight back and through along the target line. For a longer shot, widen your stance and hold the club at the end of the grip. For a shorter shot, narrow your stance and choke down on the club.

Playing the Sprinter

This shot will carry about halfway to the hole and run the rest of the way along the ground. Play the ball back in your stance. Again, we intend this to mean "back" in relation to center. Play the ball about 2 inches to the right of the center of your body. This will put your hands out in front of the clubhead and the ball. The shaft of the club will be leaning toward the target, reducing the effective loft of the club.

This is a little bit of change-up here, so pay attention: Set your feet, knees, and hips so they're aimed parallel to a line that runs from the ball to a point slightly left of the target. Here's the tricky part: Set your shoulders along a line aimed slightly right of the target. Aim your shoulders to the right of the target the same amount you set the rest of your body to the left of the target.

Swing along your shoulder line. For a longer shot, widen your stance and grip the club at the top. For a shorter shot, narrow your stance and choke down on the club.

The Common Mistakes of Pitching

Screwing up what seems like a simple pitch shot can be absolutely maddening. Nothing chafes at the mind like being in position to hit one stiff only to watch in horror as you lay the sod over it or catch the ball with the lead edge and send it screaming across the green. Or, worse yet (and dare we say it?), watching in disbelief and muttering expletives as the ball goes sideways—the much despised shank. If you're having trouble playing effective pitch shots, check for these things which might indicate your short game is leaking oil.

Clubface Is Aimed Left or Right

This is a common error, which in its simplest form can lead to pulled and pushed shots, and in its exaggerated form can lead to shanks. Our advice on how to avoid this is to always get the clubface aimed and set before you make any body adjustments. In other words, pick your target and aim the club first. As long as you're not in a hazard or a bunker, ground the club behind the ball and let the top of the shaft lean against your left hand while you aim the rest of your body. Take the time to do this because it may resolve your inconsistencies regarding accuracy. More often than not, problems with shot direction stem from the setup.

Top of the Grip Isn't Pointing at the Center of Your Body

If you lay the sod over one, there's a good chance it is because you have the butt of the club pointed to the left of the center of your body. When you do this, your hands are way too far ahead of the ball and you bring the club down toward the ball at far too steep an angle. When you have the butt of the club pointed to the right of the center of your body, it should feel exceedingly uncomfortable unless you're double jointed. Beyond that, you'll have set your wrists at an angle precisely the opposite of the angle you want. You'll almost certainly hit the ball thin and maybe fat, depending on your timing. Always take a quick check to see that the butt of the club is pointing at the center of your body.

Overlooking the Shift in Ball Position

If you play the ball too far back in your stance it's highly likely that you'll hit the ground with the club before you strike the ball. If you play the ball too far forward, you'll catch the ball skinny. Whenever you get a case of the "fats" or the "thins," the first thing you should check is the position of the ball in relation to your body.

Swinging Club Along the Target Line

If you're attempting to play the Biter or the Sprinter, we've told you to set your body lines at different targets than the clubface, and to swing along your shoulder line. If you swing down along the target line when your shoulders are aimed left of the target, you'll push the shot to the right. In a worst-case scenario, you could shank the ball. If you swing down the target line when your shoulders are aimed right of the target, you'll pull the shot to the left. You could possibly hit this one fat.

Spin City

Being able to spin the ball on the green is like having money: If it comes easy to you then you don't know what all the fuss is about. And if it doesn't come easy to you, then it's a real puzzle trying to figure how other people get it. To be able to use spin to your advantage, it helps to know how it's created.

The first thing to know about spin is that the harder you hit the ball, the more it will spin. If you want to get really technical, you'd say the harder you hit the ball, the more revolutions per second the ball makes in the air. The thing that makes spinning your short shots more difficult is that you're not making a full swing, and as a result you're not hitting the ball as hard as you can. That is the main reason that good players like you should always lay up to distances where you can hit a full wedge. If you can make a full swing with your wedge, you're halfway to playing a shot with enough backspin that you'll notice it.

The single biggest key to hitting shots with backspin is to catch the ball cleanly at impact. You must hit the ball first and the ground second. In other words, you must place the clubface directly on the back of the ball. To accomplish this, play the ball in the middle of your stance and set up with most of your weight on your left leg. Having your weight on your front leg will help create a more upright (up and down) swing, which will make it easier to make a clean strike on the ball. When you swing the club, turn your body as you do when playing other shots, but don't shift your weight to your right foot—leave it on your left side throughout the entire swing.

Generally speaking, you're safe using backspin when the hole is cut on a flat part of the green, or a part of the green that is sloping away from you. You don't want to put backspin on the ball when the hole is cut near any slopes on the green that lean toward you. Think about how many times you've seen tour players hit a ball on a green and then watched as the ball came spinning back off the green. You'll see this a lot during the Masters, where there are a lot of greens with sharply sloping fronts. You should understand that if a tour player doesn't want to spin the ball to a hole position that slopes toward him, then you don't either.

THE DIFFERENCE MAKERS

There is a noticeable difference between being competent at something and excelling at it. There is a difference between having a short game that will pull you through under "typical" circumstances and one that will win the day for you no matter what situations you face. That difference is in the details—things such as being able to precisely control the length of a shot, be it a 70-yard wedge shot or a 32-foot chip. In fact, being able to control the distance a shot carries and correctly predicting how it will react once it hits the ground are the key points in playing what we'll call "partial shots." What we mean by "partial" is that the distance calls for less than a full swing—a half swing or a three-quarter swing. And, yes, you can put effective backspin on partial shots, too—under the right conditions.

Having full control over your partial wedge shots has a dramatic impact on your scores because so many of the shots you face during a round are partial shots. It's not exactly a secret, but most poor players never get the hang of playing these partial shots. So in a sense it can be a secret weapon for you if it's something you know how to do and other players don't. Here's a list of short game shots and strategies that can make the difference between a score of 85 and a score of 95.

The Three-Quarter Wedge Shot

This is a shot you probably need four or five times during a typical round. Actually, you need it any time you're closer than a full wedge, but still have too far to cover for it to be a "feel" shot. The first thing you need to know about playing a three-quarter wedge shot is that there is nothing abbreviated about it. It has a clear beginning and end, and if you cut either part short, you're not going to like the result. In essence what we're doing here is pointing out the downside before we tell you how to play the shot. That's because the greatest number of mis-hits in attempting this shot occur because the player cuts the swing off before it's finished.

Allow us a little sidenote on that subject. There are an awful lot of players out there who confuse partial wedge shots with "punch" shots. There's a good reason for this: A punch shot is one of the easiest shots to execute in golf. It involves a short backswing and crisp feel at impact, and it has no follow-through. So, the punch shot is easy to execute and it feels good. It's also a basically useless shot unless you're playing out from the trees to get your ball back in play. It's difficult to judge the distance a punch shot will carry, and it won't have any backspin on it. The reason for the confusion is that players hear or read the words "partial swing" and their brain says, "punch shot," because of the lack of follow-through on a punch shot and because it's one shot almost every golfer knows how to play. Well, if you're 80 yards from the green and you take your wedge and slam it down on the back of the ball with no follow-through, one of two things will happen: You'll either hit way behind the ball and take a divot the size of Rhode Island, or you might catch the ball clean. And if, by some miracle, you catch the ball clean and have guessed correctly about how hard to hit it, you're still out of luck, because when the ball hits the green it's going to bounce over the back of the green. All that by way of saying do not confuse these partial shots with punch shots.

When playing a three-quarter wedge shot, the first thing to focus on is the fact that you are going to do more than just swing your arms back and forth. Even though this isn't a full swing, you still need to make the ball fly a fair distance. You have to get your body into the act. You're not going to make a huge body turn as you would with your driver, but you do want to execute a smooth, rotating swing that allows you to keep the club under control.

There are two things to key on during your setup: Play the ball in the center of your stance (remember to use your body as your reference point and not your feet) or maybe even slightly to the right of center. And you want to maintain a relationship between the butt of the club and the center of your body throughout the swing. That second part is important. When you address the ball it's no problem to have the butt of the club pointing at the center of your body, but as you turn your shoulders and, indeed, your entire upper body, this can be a little tricky if you think of this relationship solely in terms of point-

Picture your arms and club as the hands of a large clock to dial up the correct swing for a partial wedge shot.

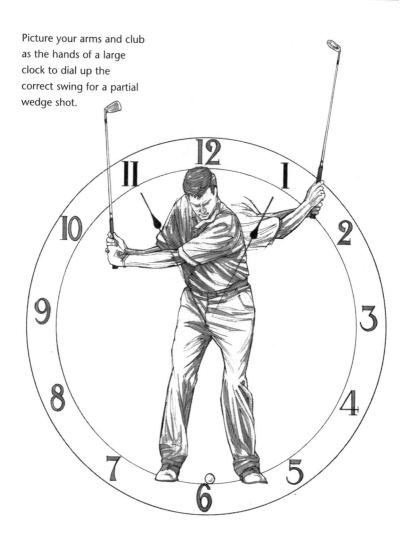

ing the butt of the club at the center of your body. That's why we say you want to "maintain the relationship" instead of something more specific.

The basic swing length for a three-quarter wedge is the 11-to-1 swing. What we mean by that is that you should picture yourself as a giant clock. Your head is 12 o'clock and your feet are 6 o'clock. So the ball and the club are at 6 o'clock as you prepare to play the shot. What you're aiming for with this shot is to swing the clubhead back to 11 o'clock and through to 1 o'clock. It's important to make the distinction between swinging the clubhead that distance and swinging your hands that distance. If you swing your hands up to 11 o'clock you'd be making a bigger swing than you normally would playing a full wedge. Nevertheless, just to get the clubhead to 11 o'clock you'll have to turn your hips and shoulders. This is the point at which you want to maintain the butt of the club/body-center relationship. If it helps, you can think about your hands instead of the butt of the club. All we're really talking about here is keeping your hands in time with your body turn. The best way to monitor this is to keep your hands in the same position relative to the center of your body from address and throughout the swing as you turn away from and through the ball. When you follow through, turn your body through and swing the clubhead up to 1 o'clock. This will produce a shot that flies shorter than a full wedge, but it will still have spin on it if played from the fairway.

Using this 11-to-1 method, you can practice creating shots that carry different distances by making small adjustments in how far you swing the club in relation to 11 o'clock and 1 o'clock. The key is to always swing the club back and through the same distance. There's a good reason for this: The natural inclination when hitting a partial shot is to attempt to add a little extra "hit" through impact, especially if you're not used to playing this shot. The fear is that the ball won't travel far enough, so you try to give it a little added oomph at impact. When you swing the same distance back and through, the club accelerates at a perfect pace due to the weight of the clubhead and the leverage you create with your body turn and the cocking of your wrists. You'll have all the clubhead speed you need without adding anything extra. In fact, attempting to hit the ball a little "harder" at impact is just going to screw you up. There is no reason to think "hit" with this shot. Think about making a syrupy smooth swing.

The Half Wedge

Still using your giant clock, you should also practice and familiarize yourself with playing a half wedge. This would be a swing where the clubhead goes from 9-to-3 on your clock. It will produce a shot longer and higher than any chip you could play. It's the shot you want to have in your bag for situations where you need a 40-yard shot, plus or minus a few yards. You can factor in those plus or minus yards by making adjustments in swing length in relation to 9 o'clock and 3 o'clock.

Practice to develop "touch." One of the great myths in golf is that a player is born with great touch and that it cannot be developed. We don't believe that and neither should you. Earlier in this book we suggested a practice session with a friend helping out so that you could determine precisely how far you hit your irons. A spin on that we'd like to suggest now is that you do the same—minus the friend—to help you determine how long a swing you need to hit any partial shot that you might face out on the course. Pace off some distances—30 yards, 40 yards, 50 yards—from the point where you'll be hitting your practice balls. Drop some towels or ball baskets at these points. Practice playing these partial shots, noting how far you have to swing the club back and through to achieve each distance. Focus on where the ball lands. Then start hitting balls to the midway point between each marker—35 yards, 45 yards—and 5 yards beyond the last marker. Again, pay attention to the length of your swing so that on the golf course you know exactly how far to swing the club.

The trajectory on any of these partial shots is determined by three things: the force of the blow, the position of the ball in your setup, and the angle of the clubface at address (and, as a result, impact). The reason you'd want to control the trajectory of the shot could be anything from wanting to keep the ball low into the wind or low because you'd like it to land into an upslope on a green and take a hop forward. You might want to hit the ball high when the hole is sitting on a downslope. In such a situation, a high shot presents you the best opportunity of getting the ball near the hole. The more precise you get with yardage control, the more apparent the situations will become where you'll want to tweak the trajectory of the shot. The longer your swing and the faster the club is moving, the higher the ball is going to fly. You can make swings of equal lengths but with different speeds by adjusting the tempo at which you swing. A slightly more upbeat tempo will produce more club-head speed. An extreme example of this can be seen in the fabulous flop shots played by Phil Mickelson on Tour. He makes a long swing but with a slow tempo, thereby adding "soft" height to the shot.

The second trajectory control factor is ball position. This is straightforward: The more forward you put the ball in your stance, the higher and softer it will fly. Move it back in your stance to produce lower, crisper shots.

The clubface element of trajectory is set at address. An open clubface produces a higher, softer shot that won't run very much. A closed clubface produces lower shots that run more.

Keep your body "quiet," then "active." When you play a pitch shot, you're going to have a certain amount of body turn. The longer the shot, the more your hips and shoulders must turn. The way of thinking of your turn during these partial shots is to think about a "quiet" turn away from the ball, and an "active" turn through the ball. This is true especially with your hips and lower body. When you swing the club back, the focus is mainly on your shoulder turn and arms as they produce the swing arc (length) and leverage necessary to produce distance. In the downswing, the lower body becomes more active. You want to lead with your hips with your arms trailing, keeping your hands well out "in front" of the clubhead. (By that we mean the clubhead never passes your hands in the race to the ball.) This sequence, "quiet, then active," often gets reversed by players who aren't sure about what they are doing. They have lots of lower body action swinging back—hips and knees are flying every which way—and then they thunk down on the ball with the arms only. That's the whole "hit" and "punch shot" mentality we were talking about earlier. Don't do it.

6

GETTING
OFF THE
BEACH

For a player of your skill level, sand is not the enemy. In fact, to a large degree it is easier to control a shot played from a greenside bunker than to play a shot of similar length from the rough. In your quest to shoot a score better than 90, you cannot be content with simply getting out of the sand. It's true that under certain circumstances simply getting the ball out of the bunker will be your only realistic play. You should accept that fate when it occurs, but more often than not you will have a chance to get the ball close to the hole. Don't settle for just getting the ball out of the sand. We say you should be greedy—you're going to have to get up and down from the sand a few times if you want to break 90.

Being an above average bunker player is a matter of two basic things: knowing how to execute the various types of shots, and knowing when to play the various types of shots.

Would you like to know the fastest way to take several strokes off your game? Spend two hours in a bunker. . . .

— *Greg Norman*

The nuances of selecting the proper shot to play are what separate the good sand player from the player who is happy just to get the ball anywhere on the green.

We'll start this chapter by reviewing the fundamentals of playing greenside bunker shots. The primary fundamental of playing out of the sand is to have a sand wedge in your bag. We're going to assume you have one of those, otherwise you wouldn't be on the cusp of breaking 90.

The Fundamentals of Playing from the Sand

For the purposes of this discussion on the fundamentals of sand play, we'll assume that you have a clean lie in the sand. We know that is not always the case, and we'll cover that later. But for the time being, you have a clean lie.

The first thing you do before entering the bunker is determine how far you want the ball to carry when executing the bunker shot. In general, the closer the ball is to the hole, the higher and shorter you want the ball to fly. As the hole moves farther away from the ball, you want to start thinking about a shot that flies lower and carries farther.

The higher the shot you wish to produce, the more open you want the clubface to be in relation to your body. The lower you want the ball to fly, the more square you want the clubface. It is important here not to confuse "opening" the clubface with aiming it to the right of the target. The thing you actually "open" is your body. You should always leave the lead edge of the club aimed at your target. (And, for the zillionth time in this book, we'll remind you that your target is not the hole, but the spot where you want the ball to land.)

As you do with every other shot in golf, you should choose your target before addressing the ball. In this case, you'll want to case the green before entering the bunker. This is because most bunkers have some sort of facing to them that will prevent you from having a full view of the putting surface. Since you might not be able to see your target as you make your swing, you want to establish a target before entering the bunker. Specifically, you want to determine how far you want the ball to fly and what kind of trajectory you want on it. What you should do is pick a spot on the lip of the bunker over which you'd like your ball to fly. Pick out some sort of distinguishing mark at that spot and then proceed into the bunker. That spot is the point at which you should aim the lead edge of your clubface. If you want to open your body in relation to your target and the clubface, make certain you open your shoulders, hips and feet—not just any single component on its own.

Once you're in the sand you want to get your feet set in position to play the shot. You probably already wiggle your feet back and forth to "dig in" somewhat, and you certainly see professionals do this on tour. This shouldn't be an absent-minded process that you do simply because it's fun to wiggle your feet around in the sand. What you're actually doing when you dig your feet into the sand is lowering yourself in relation to the ball. How far down you dig with your feet and how close you stand to the ball are inextricably linked. When you want to play a high shot, you want to stand farther away from the ball and also have feet dug farther down into the sand. The farther you stand from the ball and the more you dig in, the steeper the resultant angle of your swing will be. When you want to hit a high soft shot, you want the club to approach the ball from a steep angle. The higher the shot you wish to produce, the

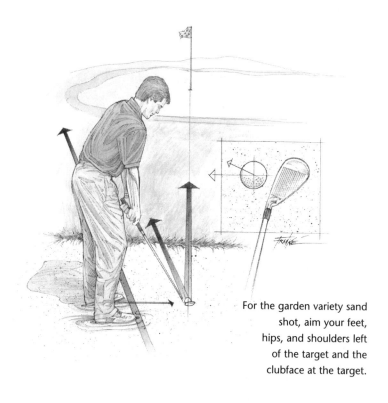

For the garden variety sand
shot, aim your feet,
hips, and shoulders left
of the target and the
clubface at the target.

steeper the angle of approach should be. Hence, the steeper you want the angle of approach to be, the farther you should stand from the ball and the more you should dig in. And the farther you stand from the ball and the more you dig in, the wider apart you should set your feet.

How far you dig into the sand with your feet and how far you stand from the ball should be proportionate to each other. If you dig down into the sand an inch with your feet, you should stand an inch farther away from the ball than you would for a normal wedge shot. Also proportionate to these things is how far down on the shaft you grip the club. The farther back you stand from the ball and the farther down you dig your feet, the more you want to choke down on the club, thereby shortening the length of the club as you move the ground "closer" to your hands.

The opposite of this is also true in that if you wish to play a lower, longer shot you should stand closer to the ball than normal and not dig your feet in quite so much.

THE PACE OF YOUR SWING FROM THE SAND

The pace at which you swing the club on a greenside bunker shot determines the amount of velocity a shot has on it, and also the amount of backspin. So when the ball is close to the hole, you want to open your body in relation to the clubface and target and choke down a few inches on the shaft. You also want to move back from the ball, dig in more with your feet, and swing at a fairly slow pace. When the hole is what you might call a medium distance from the ball, you want to stand pretty much square to the clubface, stand the normal distance from the ball that you would for any wedge shot, and swing at a medium pace. When you want to produce a lower, longer shot, stand closer to the ball, don't dig in at all with your feet, and swing the club at a slightly quicker pace back and through.

THE NUANCES OF BEING A GREAT SAND PLAYER

Every sand shot is different, so everything you've read prior to this point in this chapter is meant to provide you with a baseline knowledge of how to handle shots from the sand. Knowing how to assess each shot and then making the necessary adjustments in your setup and stance is what will make you a great sand player.

The process of assessing the shot begins with a close examination of the lie. There are three types of lie you can get in the sand: the normal lie, the fried egg, and the buried lie. What we call a normal or typical lie is when the ball is sitting cleanly atop the sand. This is the type of lie you normally get when a ball bounces on the ground before entering the bunker. That bounce on the ground takes a lot of the heat off the ball, so it sort of skips softly into the bunker. The result is that the ball doesn't really penetrate the sand. It just sits on top of it.

> *I have said before that too much ambition is a bad thing to have in a bunker. . . .*
>
> *— Bobby Jones*

The fried egg usually occurs only when the ball flies directly into the bunker. It's called a fried egg because sand immediately surrounding the ball is dispersed in a circular pattern. The ball is fully visible, but there is no sand immediately touching the ball on the sides. It resembles a sunny-side up egg, hence the name.

A ball is considered buried when only the top half or less is visible. The sand does not disperse as it does with the fried egg—the ball slams into the sand, usually from a high trajectory, and plugs deep into the sand. In many cases this happens when the ball lands directly in the face of the bunker. The faces of bunkers tend to have more sand covering them than the flat parts of the bunker. If the sand is soft, the ball buries in the sand and creates a shot of greater difficulty.

Once you've made an assessment of your lie, you're ready to pick a target for your shot. From a clean lie and from some fried egg lies, you have every opportunity to play a shot in which you have excellent control of the height and distance and the amount the ball will roll. From some fried egg lies and all buried lies, your options are limited. A buried lie forces you to play an explosion shot, and it's difficult to judge how far an explosion shot will run once it hits the green. The determining factor about which type of shot you can play from a fried egg is how much sand is directly behind the ball—the point where the club will enter the sand. We'll cover this more in a bit, because where the club enters the sand behind the ball depends on what type of shot you want to play.

Splash or Explode: The Two Basic Shots

There are two basic types of shot you can play from the sand: the splash shot and the explosion shot. Each can be tweaked to some degree to produce different heights and lengths. The splash shot can also have various amounts of spin. You're out of luck when it comes to trying to spin the ball from a buried lie with the explosion shot.

The first rule of selecting between the two shots is an easy one: Play the splash shot whenever you can. One of the problems we frequently see in our schools among players who can't break 100 or 90 on a regular basis is that they play every sand shot as if it were an explosion shot. Somewhere, somehow they came to the conclusion that every bunker shot is an explosion shot. Perhaps it's because they never had the patience to practice the technique for playing the splash shot. It is true that the explosion shot is slightly easier to play, but it doesn't allow you to get the ball anywhere near the hole by any means other than luck. The reason you want to play the splash shot at every opportunity is that you increase spin and control on your shot by limiting the amount of sand that gets between the clubface and the ball. The more sand you dig up, the less control you have over the shot.

A splash shot is the type of shot that the sand wedge was invented to play. You can use any club to hit an explosion shot, but a splash shot requires a club that will gently deflect off the sand after penetrating the surface. The idea is to skim through a thin layer of sand behind and underneath the ball. To the poor player, this is certainly a more dangerous shot to play. In your case, however, you're ready to take the step up and learn to play this shot effectively.

One of the primary elements of executing this shot is trust—that is, trust in your sand wedge. If you're not used to playing this type of shot, you might want to start out using a sand wedge that has more bounce. Eventually, the better you get at the shot, the less bounce you'll want on your sand wedge. This is because as you continue improving your ability to hit this shot, you'll want the club to enter the sand closer and closer to the ball. In any case, in terms of trust, you have to rely on the club to deflect up once it hits the sand.

All through this book we've encouraged you not to use your feet as your reference point for anything in your setup. This is another case where we'd like you to focus on that. Since the width of your stance is going to vary depending on the type of shot you play, you should continue to use your body (or more specifically, your chest) as your main reference point. In the case of playing the splash shot, you want to play the ball forward in your stance. Somewhere about equal with your left armpit will do nicely as a starting point. You can make adjustments as you go along. Once you have this set, open your body up to the target line while keeping the clubface aimed at your target. When you swing the club, swing it along the straight lines of your body, not along the target line. The effect this creates is that of the club "cutting across" the ball.

When you swing the club back you want to make sure you keep your lower body quiet. One way of doing this is to set up

To become a better bunker player, you must remember to hit through the ball, not at it. To hit the ball higher and farther, complete the swing to a full, high follow-through.

with your weight mostly on your left leg and to leave it there throughout the entire swing. Even when your shoulders turn away from the ball in the backswing, you leave the weight on your left leg.

There are two things about this shot that make it seem difficult to players who are not used to executing it. The first thing is the path of the swing, and the second is the length of the follow-through. The swing path problem is not all that different than the one posed when playing pitch shots. You simply swing the club along the lines where your body is aimed. In almost every case when you're playing a splash shot, that is going to be a point left of the target.

The second sticky point about playing the splash shot is the length of the follow through. This point is the boogie man of golf. The reason so many average players are horrible from the sand is because they are terrified to maintain the speed of the club through the sand and to swing to a full follow-through position. This fear is instinctive and, to some degree at least, logical. The fear is that if you make a solidly paced swing with a big follow-through, the ball is going to go too far. That's not going to happen. Another reason that players struggle with the length of the follow-through is that the splash shot is by nature a gentle shot, the distance of which is controlled in large part by the length of the backswing. To produce a very short shot, the club has to be swung back only a short distance in the backswing. However, the hands must still swing through to head high during the follow-through. This disproportionate swing seems to mess with the minds of borderline players. There is only one way to overcome this fear: Practice these shots until you become familiar with the unbalanced swing length and the close proximity of the clubhead to the ball at impact.

The explosion shot is an altogether different kettle of fish from the splash shot. There is more than one situation where you might want to play an explosion shot. When your ball is buried, you have no choice—you must play an explosion shot. When you have a severe fried egg, that is, the sand around the ball has vanished to the point that there is no sand directly behind the ball at the point you'd like the club to enter the sand, then you should probably opt for the explosion shot rather than risk blading the ball across the green. The third time you might want to play an explosion shot is when you are in a front bunker at a very large, deep green, and the hole is cut in the back of the green. In such a situation, it can be difficult to fly the ball to the precise point you would need to, and as a result you might end up overswinging or catching too little sand and sending the ball flying over the green. The explosion shot, which runs quite a bit once it hits the ground, can come in handy at such moments.

How much the ball runs once it's on the putting surface depends on a few factors: how hard you swing, the club you use (it's not automatically a sand wedge), how close to the ball you slam the club into the sand, and the type of sand in the bunker. (More on the type of sand in a moment.)

The fundamental moves for playing the explosion shot are as follows:

• The primary goal and therefore the thing you should focus on with this shot is digging the club down into the sand. *This is clearly the opposite of the splash shot.* Here you are using the clubhead almost as a shovel. The least resistance occurs when you dig into the sand with the lead edge of the clubface square to the target line. The idea is for the club to dig underneath and behind the ball and for the resulting forward-moving explosion of sand to lift the ball up onto the green. There is no spin on this shot because too much sand gets between the clubface and the ball.

- Since you want the clubface to be square to the target line, we recommend playing this shot from a perfectly square stance. If you open your stance as you do for a splash shot, you might end up yanking the shot horribly to the left or leaving it in the bunker.
- Since you want the club to approach the ball at quite a steep angle and to hit into the sand behind the ball, you'll want to position the ball at least as far back as the inside of your right shoulder. The deeper the ball is buried, the farther back in your stance you want it at address.
- You want to lean your body toward the target when playing this shot. Set up to the ball with most of your weight on your left leg and feeling as if your head is well ahead of the ball. Keep those two feelings throughout your swing.
- The swing itself is a pure hatchet job. Since you have the ball back in your stance you're going to be lifting the clubhead almost straight into the air. The closer to the ball you strike the sand, the more the ball should carry. The danger here is that if you hit too close to the ball, you may end up leaving the ball in the sand because you haven't displaced enough sand to lift the ball into the air. Along those same lines, if you hit too far behind the ball, you'll put too much sand between your club and the ball, and the "explosion" will occur too far behind the ball. The result is that the ball stays in the sand. The only way to get a feel for how close to drive the club into the sand is to practice by pushing balls into the sand at varying depths, say three-quarters buried, top of ball level with top of sand, and top of ball actually below the top of the sand.
- There is no follow-through on this shot. It's not because you wouldn't want to follow through, it's because it's impossible to do so due to the angle at which the club strikes the sand.
- The club selection on this shot is really a judgment call on your part. The deeper the ball in the sand, the more difficult it

To extricate your ball from a buried lie, you must dig the clubhead into the sand. Take a deep, vertical path to the ball, slam the leading edge of the clubhead into the sand behind the ball, and take little or no follow-through.

is to force the sand wedge down far enough to extricate the ball. You might want to opt for the pitching wedge, which depending on what type of irons you play may have a "sharper" or thinner leading edge, ideal for digging deeper into the sand. You may even want to try an 8-iron or 9-iron depending on how far you'd like the ball to run after it hits the green. If you want extra run to a back pin, the 8-iron or 9-iron could do the trick. Maximum loft is not so important in playing the explosion shot as it is in playing the splash shot.

The X Factors in Playing from the Sand

Life is filled with X factors, those monkey-wrench variables that can take your absolute rules and turn them inside out and upside down. Putting is probably the only part of golf that has as many X factors as playing from the sand. Spotting the variables in sand play is a little bit like being a detective looking for clues. They aren't at all obvious and you have to know where to look or you'll come up empty.

Here's a list of things to consider when playing from the sand. They aren't in any particular order because they don't occur in any particular order. It's just a list of things to look for.

- When hitting a splash shot you get maximum control over spin and distance by taking as little sand as possible. How much sand you take, however, depends on what kind of sand is in the bunkers. The things to look for in sand are texture (small grains or big grains), weight (light or heavy), and moisture.
- Generally speaking, if the sand looks like big granules, it will be a little loose. If it looks really fine, it's going to be a little heavier. This means that in big-grained sand, when it's dry, you don't have to swing as hard. When the sand feels fine and your feet sink into it when you walk on it, you're going to have to swing harder. You can still hit close to the ball to get the spin, but you're going to have to pick up the pace of your swing. Dry, heavy beachlike sand absorbs the blow more, so you have to swing a little harder. In this type of sand, if the ball is sitting in any sort of depression, you're probably better off playing an explosion shot.
- Sand becomes more compact when it gets a healthy dose of rain. If there has been enough rain to compact the sand, the

wet sand is going to be an excellent transmitter of energy. That means you don't have to swing as hard as you normally would for a shot of whatever length you face. You also have to hit closer to the ball when the sand is wet.

- Lighter-colored sand tends to be lighter in weight and texture, and dry out quicker when it gets wet. Darker sand tends to be heavier (swing harder) and hold moisture more (swing easier). How's that for confusing? You have to make a determination if the dark sand is wet. Which quality will dominate? Probably the wetness.

- In bunkers exposed to a dominant wind flow, the light stuff will blow away. So what's left will be a little heavier and of a heavier grain.

- Listen to the sound your feet make when you're walking into the bunker. If it sounds crunchy it means it's granular and hard, so swing easy. If it sounds muffled and feels squishy, you'll want to swing a little harder.

- If the wind has been blowing really hard and what's left of the sand seems extremely hard, you might want to use your pitching wedge. Your sand wedge might bump off the surface and the lead edge of the club will catch the center of the ball. You know what happens then.

- The closer you hit to the ball and the more you cut across it (the more open your body is in relation to the target line), the more the ball is going to spin. You should consider this when selecting a target.

- If there is water or out-of-bounds or any other hazard behind the pin, reduce the chances of hitting the ball long by taking more sand and picking a target well short of the hole.

- If the ball gets caught up on a downslope, you can still get the ball out. Lean with the hill and play the ball back in your stance. Try to hit as close to the ball as you can. If there is any trouble behind the hole—say water or another bunker—play to a part of the green that is safe. The ball will come out lower, but if you catch it clean it should have a little spin on it.

- If the ball is severely buried in the face and you confront a steep lip, it's going to be tough to get the ball up and over the lip. Look for a spot where the lip is a little lower, or for a spot that you can play out of sideways.

7

CONTROLLING
BALL
FLIGHT

A good golf course is meant to fully test every aspect of your game. That means the greens on a good course will have sections that are less accessible than other sections—areas that will force you to carry or flirt with a hazard in order to get the ball close to the hole. In other cases, a hole may call for the tee shot to be placed on a particular side of the fairway in order to have the best angle of approach to the green. If you do not possess the ability to produce shots that curve while in flight, you're letting the course architect beat you. If you can only make the ball curve one way or generally hit the ball straight, there are going to be times when you cannot exploit the preferred avenues of approach on a given hole. Certain flag positions will be hidden from you, and you'll have to lay back on certain tee shots where you could otherwise take a more aggressive line.

The quality of being able to maneuver the ball in flight is known as "working the ball," and it is an element of playing that you should strive to include in your game. The quest to break 90 every time out means that a single shot here and there can make the difference. And why settle for 88 when you could shoot 84 if you could attack a few more pin positions? This chapter is going to teach when and how to work the ball.

Why Work the Ball?

Golf is not a game that rewards unnecessary risks and silly thoughts. There isn't any point to just curving the ball back and forth, or hitting it high or low, if you don't get some sort of tangible bonus from doing so.

The first place it will reward you is a result of the way a golf course is set up. They don't cut every hole on the right side of the green, nor do they cut every hole on the left side of the green. In the same manner, the various holes call for you to place your tee shots on different sides of a hole.

Why not just hit it straight all the time, you might ask? Well, if you can hit the ball straight every time, you're wasting your time reading a book by a couple of hacks like us, because we can't hit the ball straight every time. When you can effectively work the ball, you give yourself a better chance of getting the ball to end up where you want it. If you set up to curve the ball a certain way and you pull it off, you're in good shape. If you don't pull it off, more than likely you'll hit it straight. It doesn't work out this way every time, but the odds are pretty good in your favor.

Let's try an example to make things a little more clear. Assuming you've used the methods described earlier in the book, you have a 9-iron in your hand and the hole is cut on the middle left of a green. If you can draw the ball—curve it just a little bit from right to left—you have a decent chance of getting the ball close to the hole without increasing your risk at all. What you do is aim at the middle of the green. If you execute the draw perfectly, you knock it stiff. If you hit the ball straight, you have a 20-footer. And it's unlikely you'll hang it out to the right. As we said, it does happen, but not all that often.

Right there you learned the first rule of working the ball: Never aim at a point where, if you hit the ball straight, you'll end up in trouble. Always aim at a spot where the result will be just fine if you hit the ball straight. In fact, you're almost always right when you decide to aim at the middle of the green. In the above example, even if you push the ball you'll just have a fairly long putt.

Another reason you want to be able to control the ball in flight has to do with the depth of the hole position on the green. If the pin is in the back, you can bring the ball in low and it has a chance to bounce back to the hole. If it holds when it hits, then you have a medium range putt. Same goes for a pin in the front of the green. If you bring it in high and beyond the hole, it might spin back to the hole. If it holds, you still have a run at a makeable putt. In both cases, the controlled shot is less risky than flying the ball right at the hole.

GETTING YOUR MIND PREPARED TO WORK THE BALL

The first mental matter to settle when you work the ball is that you're going to make it all happen with your setup. You may have previously heard or read about methods for working the ball that involve changing your swing plane for various shots or other like-minded stuff. We say that's balderdash. Everything you need to do can be accomplished in your setup.

The second mental key is to take an extra few seconds during your pre-shot routine to see the shot in your mind. This probably isn't the first time you've heard about visualization techniques, but the reality is that very few players bother to try to see each shot in their mind before they play it. It would get a little tiresome if you tried to see every shot before you hit it, and it would take away from the time you spend busting your buddies' chops. We recommend it in any situation when you want to work the ball because it really helps. If you picture the ball in flight for just a second—or just picture a curving arrow just like in a golf magazine—it will help you make the good swing you want to make. Try it. If you think we're full of hooey, you'll probably still be able to work the ball just fine. It might help, however.

Your Follow-Through Holds the Key

This is a bit backwards, but we think it will help you create shots if you understand the follow-through position for each type of shot before you attempt to start working the ball. It's the old idea that if the club finishes where it's supposed to, then you must have done a good job with your swing prior to that point. A full follow-through is important on any shot, but when you're working the ball your goal is to achieve very specific follow-through positions. If you set up to the ball properly and achieve these follow-through positions, you will pull your shot off nine times out of ten. Those positions are:

- When you want to hit a fade—a shot that curves from left to right—the shaft of the club (and the clubhead) should be pointing to the right as you hold your follow-through position.
- When you're attempting to play a draw (right to left), the shaft of the club should be pointing to the left as you hold your follow-through.

- If you want to hit the ball high in the sky, finish with your hands high—up near your head.
- If you want to play a low shot, finish with your hands low in comparison to a normal follow-through. About chest high is as far as they should go.

You'll still need to make some adjustments to your setup, but once you do, if you swing through to these follow-through positions, you'll be in good shape.

Setting Up to Play the Fade and the Draw

The adjustments in your setup to play either a fade or a draw are actually quite simple. Like almost every other shot, you want the clubface aimed directly at the target, that is, the point where you want the ball to finish up. This is the same for both the fade and the draw.

When you want to play a fade, set your body lines (shoulders, hips, feet) so that they are aimed at the point where you'd like the ball to start curving back toward the target. In this case, since the fade moves from left to right, you'd set your body lines aimed at a point to the left of the target. (Don't confuse this with the point we made earlier in the book about how for a normal shot you aim your body to a point that is left of, but parallel to, your target.) You do not set your body lines parallel to your target line—you aim them directly at whatever point you choose left of your target. How much the ball curves is dictated by how far you aim to the left. The more you aim to the left, the more the ball will curve.

When you want to play a draw you follow the same procedure with the exception that you aim your body to the right of the target instead of to the left of the target. Just as when you

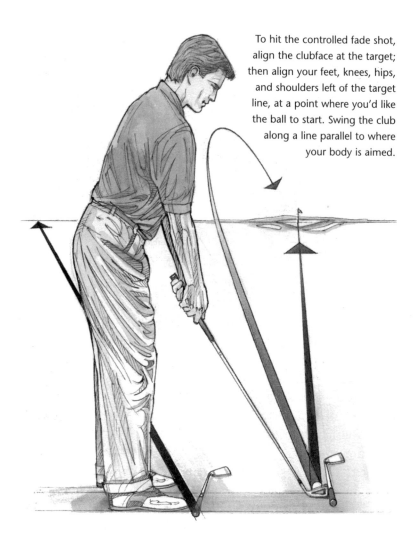

To hit the controlled fade shot, align the clubface at the target; then align your feet, knees, hips, and shoulders left of the target line, at a point where you'd like the ball to start. Swing the club along a line parallel to where your body is aimed.

hit the fade, the amount of curve on the shot is dictated by how far you aim your body away from the target. In this case, the more you aim to the right, the more the ball will curve.

Whether you're playing the fade or the draw, the basic swing thought is to swing the club along the same line your

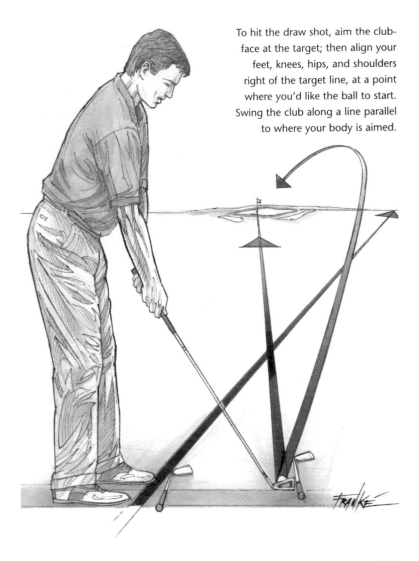

To hit the draw shot, aim the club-face at the target; then align your feet, knees, hips, and shoulders right of the target line, at a point where you'd like the ball to start. Swing the club along a line parallel to where your body is aimed.

body is aimed on. That means if you're hitting a fade, the club does not move straight back from the ball, it starts on a line outside the ball. And if you're hitting a draw, the club starts back inside the ball. Then just focus on those follow-through points we made earlier.

Here are some more points you might find useful in fading and drawing the ball:

- If you consider yourself a "feel" player, these shots are a lot of fun to play. If you have a great feel for your swing, you can make some adjustments in your grip pressure for each type of shot. For a fade, if you rate your normal grip pressure a 4 on a scale of 1 to 10, ratchet your right hand pressure up to 5 and your left hand pressure—particularly the top three fingers on the shaft—up to 7. If you start your downswing by pulling down with your left arm, that extra grip pressure in the left hand will prevent the toe of the club from turning over in front of the heel. For the draw, lighten your right hand grip pressure—especially your index finger—to a 3. And drop the left hand pressure down to a 2. This will make your wrists a little more active and make sure the clubface stays in the position you want it in.
- One final point: It's easier to fade less-lofted clubs, and easier to draw more-lofted clubs. That's not to say you can't draw a 4-iron. Just remember that it's not as easy as drawing a 9-iron.

CREATING HIGH AND LOW SHOTS

You've undoubtedly faced situations on the golf course where you would like to be able to hit the ball low. Perhaps the wind is stiff and you'd like to hit a low shot, or maybe there's a tree limb hanging over your target line and you want to be sure you sneak under it. And once in a while—but not too often—you need to hit a shot that flies higher than normal, to go over a tree for instance.

To hit the ball low requires adjustments in club selection, your setup, and your swing. The adjustments are fairly simple, however. The first adjustment is to take more club than you normally would for the distance—two more clubs to be precise. As you set up to the ball, choke down on the shaft about two inches and play the ball about one ball width farther back in your stance than you normally would with the club you've selected. Use slightly more grip pressure than you do for normal shots. You'll want to set up in a slightly open stance—shoulders, hips, and feet slightly left of parallel with your target line. This is an adjustment made necessary by the shift in ball position. Your weight distribution should favor the target side—your left leg.

When you make your swing for the low shot, shorten your backswing to about three-quarters of what it normally is with the club you're swinging. Now here's an important part: Don't just lift the club straight up and thump it on the back of the ball like you're hitting a punch shot. You're not hitting a punch shot. If you try to punch the ball you're going to create too steep an angle coming into the ball, and as a result you'll send the ball flying higher than you want. Make sure you turn your chest and shoulders back and make a regular swing—just a little shorter. Another pitfall to watch out for is swinging too hard. This too will force the ball high into the air. Your swing should come to a finish with your hands, elbows, and clubhead no higher than your shoulders.

To play a high shot, use very light grip pressure and keep your wrists loose and free of tension. Play the ball about one ball width farther forward in your stance than you normally would with the club you've selected. (If you're trying to clear a tree, make sure you've taken enough loft to easily clear the top of it.) In your setup, you'll want to tilt your upper body slightly to the right—away from the target. You should feel like your right ear is over your right knee. The key here when making the swing is to not lunge toward the target. Just make a normal swing, with full chest turn away from the ball. Make the fullest possible follow-through, with your hands ending up by your left ear and the club wrapped around behind your neck.

DEALING WITH BAD LIES

Golf is not a game of certainties, and one of the things you can never be too certain about is the lie of your ball once you've left the tee. Here is a list of situations that have an impact on the shape of the shot you're going to play, and some instructions on how to handle these situations when you encounter them.

If your ball ends up in an old divot: You'll want to pay attention to what part of the divot your ball is in, but more on that in a moment. The first rule is that regardless of where the ball sits in a divot, you'll want to stand a little closer to the ball than you normally would with the club you've chosen. This makes the club "stand up" at a more upright angle. This reduces the chances that the club will get snagged on the edges of the divot.

If the ball is sitting near the front of the divot—the part closer to your target—your goal is to sweep the ball out of the divot with your normal swing. The only change you need to

Why Down Equals Up in Ball Flight

The reason so many poor players think they have to "lift" the ball into the air is that they don't grasp the idea that in golf, down equals up. In other words, the steeper the angle at which the clubface descends into the ball, the higher the ball will fly. It doesn't seem logical, but then who ever said golf was logical?

A golf ball gets lifted into the air the same way an airplane does. There is air flow passing over and under the ball. There is more pressure underneath the ball when it is first struck, which creates some lift.

make in your setup is to move the ball about an inch forward of where you would normally play it with the club you've selected. The ball should fly fairly normally.

If the ball is sitting near the back part of the divot you're going to have to dig it out of there, so expect the ball to come out hot and running. Play the ball an inch farther back in your stance than you normally would for the club you've chosen—which should be one club more than the distance requires. Choke down about an inch on the shaft, take a three-quarter backswing and hit down hard on the back of the ball. Take an abbreviated follow-through. This shot can have a tendency to squirt to the right, so you might want to aim a little left of your target to compensate for this.

If your ball is sitting above your feet: The first rule of uneven lies is that the ball flight always matches whatever type of slope you're on. The second rule is that you always want to make a three-quarter length swing. If the ball is below your feet, it's going to curve from right to left in flight. You want to lean into the hill and keep your posture fairly erect. The way you lean into the hill without falling over is to use a little knee flex.

That's what the dimples on the ball do—help funnel that air pressure and lift the ball.

The real reason down equals up is that when you strike a downward blow at the ball it maintains contact with the clubface for a split second longer. The ball runs up the clubface (rather than being howitzered forward) and this gives the grooves on the club time to "engage" or create spin. When they make spin, the ball spins back toward the clubface—backspin. And the backspin helps lift the ball into the air even more. Got it? Good. From now on, when you want to make the ball go up, hit down.

You're going to want to aim to the right of your target—how far right depends on the severity of the hill you're on. The steeper the hill, the more the ball will curve. Play the ball about two inches to the right of center in your stance. Choke down on the shaft about one and a half inches. Make a three-quarter swing, concentrating on keeping your balance from start to finish.

If your ball is sitting below your feet: The first thing you want to do in this situation is take a wider than normal stance. You need to "lower" yourself down to the ball in this situation, which means you'll need to use some extra knee flex. Something else that will help you maintain your balance is to point both toes in toward the ball—pigeon toe yourself for a moment. Play the ball about two inches farther forward in your stance than you would with the same club from a level lie. Aim left, and allow for the ball to come out hot and squirty and moving from left to right. It's not going to have any backspin on it.

When you have an uphill lie: An uphill lie is one that forces your body to lean away from the target. Place the ball in the middle of your stance and flare your front foot toward the target. Tilt your shoulders so that they lean with the hill. Your right shoulder will be lower than your left. Use one more club than the distance calls for and aim to the right. You'll hit either a dead pull to the left or a (really) high draw.

When you have a downhill lie: This is when your body is leaning toward the target. This sucker is going to come out hot and low and curving to the right. You'll want to take one less club than the distance calls for, since the ball is going to run and you need the help of the loft in this situation. Play the ball in the middle of your stance and set your shoulders level with the slope. Your left shoulder will be lower than your right shoulder.

8

THE ICING
ON
THE CAKE

Everyone knows how to putt, right? Give a monkey a stick and a ball and tell him to knock in a three-footer to win a few skins and he could probably do it. At least that's what people who don't know how to putt think. Here's what we say: There's no excuse for not being an excellent putter. Everything about putting can be learned and, truthfully, it's rather simple stuff. You just have to put a little time into it. Everything in this book to this point has been presented with the idea of making you a smarter, more consistent striker of the ball from tee to green. Well, now you're on the green. It's time to make something happen in your game, and this is the place for it. If you can take fewer putts per round and play smarter from tee to green, you're in there like swimwear, baby—breaking 90 is a done deal.

> *The man who can putt is a match for anyone.*
>
> — *Willie Park, Jr.*

We're not going to spend a lot of time in this chapter belaboring the fundamentals of putting. We're going to give them to you straight up just in case you need a tune-up, then we're heading right into the good stuff: the super-subtle aspects of putting that will allow you to kick butt on the greens.

THE BEST WAY TO SWING THE PUTTER

You've read thousands of magazine articles, read hundreds of books, watched untold number of instructional videos and watch the Golf Channel to the point that your wife is ready to run over your clubs with her SUV. And every time you read or hear about putting, they tell you that it's the most individualized part of the game and that you can set up and swing the club any way you damned well please as long as it's square at impact. To some degree, all of that is true. But we don't want you to settle for that because you have to be a better than average putter if you're going to break 90.

Our recommendation to you is to use what is commonly called the pendulum putting stroke. If you already do, keep reading and perfect it. If you don't already use it, switch to it. If you do nothing else in this book, adopt this putting method. You'll make up the $12.95 your kids spend on this book for you a thousand times over in weekend bets. And here's why you should switch: Swinging the putter is all about maintaining a steady pace throughout the stroke. You do not accelerate the putter through the ball, you simply maintain the pace you started out with. That advice is often given to prevent players from slowing the putter down (usually out of fear), but it's not true. You want to maintain the pace of the putter's movement, and the pendulum stroke is the best way for you to do that. Other types of wristy strokes are too dangerous and will leave you susceptible to what we call "handsy explosions"—rapid changes in the pace of the putter's motion.

The best way to grasp the concept of a pendulum stroke is to watch the pendulum of a grandfather clock in action. Just watch it: back and forth, back and forth, back and forth . . . always at the same tempo. Never going faster or slower. There is no manipulation involved in it—no one is trying to make that pendulum do anything other than what it does for a living. Back and forth, back and forth, back and forth . . .

The other thing you'll notice about the clock's pendulum as it swings back and forth is that it goes back the same distance and through the same distance. Every time, time after time. It doesn't go back two inches and then suddenly lurch forward six inches. See? There's a lot you can learn from this clock thing.

> *The stroke must be made with rhythm. The change of direction should be smooth and unforced, just as it is with the pendulum of a grandfather clock.*
>
> *— Tom Watson*

And that's what the pendulum putting stroke is all about: It's acceleration without effort. Force without manipulation. Once it's moving there doesn't need to be any more energy added to it or energy taken away from it. Now let's look at how to do it.

The Perfect Stroke

The pendulum motion is upper-body-oriented without any wrist action whatsoever. All you're really going to do during the stroke is rock your shoulders back and forth. Having said that, let's dive right in and nail this thing down tight.

There are various types of grips that can be used. The reverse overlap is the most popular. That's when you take the index and middle finger of your left hand and put them over the fingers of your right hand. You can grip the club any way that feels comfortable as long as you do two things: (1) place the grip in the lifeline of your left hand, and (2) make certain that your grip allows you to keep the back of your left hand facing the target from the address position all the way through to the finish of your stroke.

As soon as you place your hands on the grip you've created a key angle. Assuming you employ a traditional placement of the hands on the club—that is, right hand on the bottom—you'll have set an angle in your right wrist. That wrist bends back slightly toward your forearm. If you can keep this angle intact throughout your stroke, you'll have eliminated any overuse of your hands in the stroke.

Always keep your grip pressure light. There's never a time when you want to squeeze the putter tight. You should be able to feel the weight of the head of the putter. That's the bottom of your pendulum—you have to be able to feel it.

We'll talk a little bit later about picking a target for your stroke, but for now what we want you to focus on is the manner in which you "step in" to your putting setup. First, aim the putter squarely down the target line. Then, step in with your body. You can square the putter with your right hand before stepping in—this will even help you set that angle we talked about. Once you step into position, align your body parallel to your target line, just like for a full swing: shoulders, hips, and feet parallel to your target line. Pay special attention to getting your shoulders squared up. Your arms follow your shoulders, and if your shoulders are pointing left of parallel to the target line, you'll swing the putter back outside the target line and then across it at impact. The result is a putt missed to the left.

If you aim your shoulders right of parallel to the target line, you're going to swing the putter from inside the target line to outside the target line, and miss the putt to the right. The goal is to swing the putter directly back and through along the target line, so make sure your shoulders are square.

Once your shoulders are set, bend forward from your hips until your eyes are directly over the ball. You want your eyes directly over the ball so when you tilt your head to look at the target, you're looking right down the chute at the target. It's best if you have your dominant eye precisely over the ball. The bend from the hips is also important. You want to make sure you bend enough so that your arms can hang straight down over the ball. If you stand up too straight, you'll yank the putter to the inside when you start it moving.

Once you've made your hip tilt, your arms should hang straight down and loose, like a swimmer on the starting block. Your hands should be directly beneath your shoulders. You've now created a triangle with your shoulders, arms and hands.

Your feet are parallel to your target line, and your weight should favor your left side. If it feels good, pinch your knees in toward the middle. This might help you feel more steady. And don't let your weight get out on the balls of your feet just because you bent forward from the waist. Keep the weight firmly in your heels.

Your ball position will be a little different for putting than for other aspects of your game. What you should do first is sole the putter on the ground so it's even with the middle of your chest. The ball goes right in front of the putter.

You're ready to make your stroke now. The top of your spine is the anchor pin, so to speak. Visualize a seesaw. Your shoulders are going to rock back and forth like a seesaw. Your spine is the point in the middle that the seesaw (your shoulders) is balanced upon.

Keep your head steady throughout the stroke. Don't move it at all. The stroke does not have any conscious "hit" to it. The club just maintains its pace and the ball gets in the way. You'll change the length of your stroke depending upon the length of a putt, but you should always swing the club back and through the same distance on a given putt. This never changes.

MAKE SURE YOU HAVE THE RIGHT PUTTER FOR YOUR STROKE

We have no idea what kind of putter you're currently using. Maybe Bobby Jones was your uncle and you're using his old Calamity Jane. Maybe you won a new titanium putter with a grape jelly insert at the Jaycees outing last month. As we said, we have no idea. And for the most part, we don't really care about what brand of putter you have—we just want to make sure you have the right type of putter. For the purposes of satisfying that demand, there are two types of putters (disregarding super-long shafted putters): center-shafted putters and rear-shafted putters. The people wielding these putters come in all shapes and sizes. Some feel comfortable bent over from the hips a lot, and some feel comfortable bending only a little.

The Pendulum Drill

Some players have a difficult time grasping the idea of the putting stroke being like a see-saw. Here's a simple drill you can try right there in your den. You do have your clubs there in the den with you, correct? Good. Take your putter and a club with a long shaft out of the bag. Place the club that isn't your putter between your arms and your torso and hold it just under your elbows. Now take your putter and

Sometimes it has to do with a person's height, sometimes with not liking to bend over. Whatever the reason may be, the fact is that if you feel like you bend over a substantial amount when putting, then you should use a putter where the shaft joins the clubhead in the center or anywhere else (maybe between the center and the heel). If you prefer to stand up a little straighter to the ball like, say, Phil Mickelson, then you're probably better off with a rear-shafted blade putter.

Another factor in making certain your putter fits you is the length of the putter. We see an awful lot of people with putters that are too long for them. Remember that we'd like you to bend forward from the hips, have your eyes over the ball, and have your arms hanging nice and loose. Considering all that, we'd like for the top of the grip of your putter to come up only to the top of your left hand when you grip the club. If your putter is too long, one of two things is going to happen: Either you're going to hold it at the top of the shaft anyway, thereby forcing tension into your arms and shoulders by bending them, or you're going to have a hunk of shaft sticking out above your hands, which will feel unwieldy and hurt your sense of feel for the clubhead. Next time you watch the tour players on television, check to see how many use putters that

start making slow, smooth strokes back and forth. If you're making a good stroke, the shaft under your arms will tilt up and down like a seesaw. Now you get it? And if the shaft pointing toward the target starts pointing left or right, then you're not moving the club straight back and straight through. In other words, you're not doing a Grade A pendulum move. Work on this drill and it will help you get the feel down pat.

If you bend significantly from the hips when putting, you should use a center-shafter putter.

aren't the perfect length for them, that is, with the shaft sticking out above their hands. The answer is zero. So if your putter is too long, ask a pro to cut the end off and stick a new grip on it for you. It will make a world of difference.

The final element of making sure the putter fits you properly is to check the lie. This is pretty simple: When you set up to a putt, the bottom of the putter should be flat on the ground. If the toe is up in the air, you need a flatter putter. If the heel is up in the air, you need a more upright lie angle. Keeping the putter flush to the ground will create a more consistent stroke.

If you stand tall when putting, you should use a rear-shafted putter.

How to Read Greens

When you start talking about reading greens, choosing a line for a putt, and getting the right amount of pace (speed) on a putt, then you're talking about the nitty-gritty of putting—the stuff that makes it possible to break 90 every time you play.

We're going to talk about getting the speed right on your putts a little later in this chapter, but for right now we're going to focus on making the right read on a putt. We need to point out, however, that you have to keep the speed of the putt in mind when assessing the break of the putt. They go hand in hand—you can't do one without the other.

Having said that, here's a big list of things that you need to be familiar with as you look over a putt attempting to get a fix on the proper line:

- When you're trying to determine the line of a putt, the thing you're looking for primarily is setting your target spot. Since most putts do not travel on a straight line to the hole, your target spot is very rarely the hole. Sometimes it is, but not too often, especially on longer putts. So your target spot on any putt that has even a little break is the highest point on the line of the break. In other words, if the putt breaks from left to right, the point where it stops moving left and starts breaking right is your target spot. Your target spot is always the highest point of the break. That's not to say that all putts break in two equal halves. No matter—the high point in your line is always the target spot. The alignment of your putter and your body, and the line of your stroke, depend entirely on finding this target spot in your line.

> *Far more putts are missed because of incorrect distance rather than incorrect direction.*
>
> *— John Jacobs*

- Your mind has to soak up a lot of information to establish your target point. That process should begin as you approach the green. Even if your ball is not on the green, you should be checking the overall setting of the green as you approach it. What you're looking for is any dominant feature of the immediate landscape. An entire green might be sitting at an angle. It helps to see that because, depending upon the severity of that angle, it could counteract some of the stuff you see on the green itself. You should also be looking for any big hills off to the sides of the greens, or be aware of the fact that the entire hole you're playing is set into the side of one huge hill. If you're playing around mountains, look for the biggest ones. All ground tends to run uphill toward them.

- The general speed of the greens is important to keep in mind as you look over a putt. On a good golf course, the speed of the greens will be consistent. The faster the greens are rolling, the more the ball will break.
- If the greens are wet from rain or early morning dew, they'll break less than normal.
- The faster a ball is moving at any given time, the less susceptible it is to break. When the ball first leaves the putter it's going to be moving fastest (except on severe downhill putts), so it's going to break less. It's always going to be moving slowest around the hole, which means it should take more break near the hole. In other words, if there is any contour near the hole, the break of the ball will be magnified at that point.
- Uphill putts break less than flat putts (they are moving slower), and downhill putts break more than flat putts.
- Putts breaking into the grain—the direction in which the grass grows—break less. Putts running with the grain break more.
- If a green looks flat, look for the lowest point on the green around the edges to get some idea of the general tilt of the green. There has to be some place for the water to run off, and the green or portions of it usually tilt in that direction.
- If a cup looks flat near the hole, take a peek in the hole and check the amount of earth poking above the hole liner. If there is the same amount of earth on all sides, the putt may be flat at the hole. If one side of the liner has more dirt showing, the putt could break from that direction as it nears the hole.
- On putts that appear to move in two or more directions, remember that the early breaks won't be as severe as the ones near the hole, when the ball is moving slower.
- The grain of the grass has a lot of effect on a putt. The type of grass generally used in warm climates is Bermuda grass.

Bermuda grass has thick blades that grow quickly after they've been cut. Bermuda likes to grow toward the setting sun, so keep in mind what direction is west while you're playing on Bermuda greens. If the grain runs across the line of your putt so that your ball breaks into the grain, this slows down your putt just as much as if you were putting dead into the grain. Dead into the grain is, of course, very slow. Downgrain putts are quick. Putts on Bermuda greens will be greatly affected by the grain as the ball loses speed. That means you have to allow for it at the hole. The way you can tell if you're downgrain is that the grass gets a kind of sheen to it—it looks shiny. If you're putting into the grain, it looks dark.

- This grain stuff is a little tricky, but if you're putting on Bermuda greens and the fringe is also Bermuda grass, there's nothing illegal about taking your putter and scraping it on the collar of the green to see which way the grass is leaning. It is against the rules to do this on the greens, however.

Perfect Putting Drills

What kind of teachers would we be if we didn't insist that you spend all of your spare time at a golf course practicing your game? Actually, we know you don't have time to burn, so we've come up with a couple of quick drills you can do for a few minutes at a time.

The speed control drill: The object of this drill is to make sure you always get the ball to the hole. What you want to do is pick a flat spot on the practice green and measure a spot about 16 inches past the hole. Take a pile of balls. As you stroke the balls, you want to focus on two things: You want to try to make every putt. But if you miss the putt, you want the ball to reach your mark 16 inches past the hole. This will help you hone your speed control.

- Bentgrass, the opposite number of Bermuda, is generally used in climates where it doesn't get extremely hot. It's a much finer blade of grass that tends to be grain free. Just remember that toward the end of the day the grass has grown some and it tends to grow toward any natural water supply in the area of the green.

We've learned from the thousands of lessons we've given at our schools that most golfers do not read enough break into putts. This might be because they don't have a routine for looking a putt over. We'd like to recommend the following routine to you:

1. Always take a look at the putt from behind the hole first. The reason for this is that the ball will be traveling at its slowest speed around the hole, so you want to get a close look at the contours around the hole.

The line control drill: Practice putting while looking at your target spot instead of at the ball. This will help you if you're loosey-goosey with your head when you putt, and you learn to focus on your target spot.

The short putt drill: You don't want to have to sweat the short ones. If you don't sweat the short ones, you'll be better on the long putts. You won't have to worry about lagging the ball into that legendary three-foot circle. (What happens if you miss the circle by three feet? You have a six-foot putt.) Try to get your long putts as close to the hole as you can. You can make the short ones routine by placing seven balls around the perimeter of the hole, each two feet from the hole. Make them all, then move your circle of balls out to three feet. If you miss one, start over.

2. Work your way back to the ball on the low side of the putt so that you can see the elevation and the slope your ball will encounter on its way to the hole.

3. Read the putt from behind the ball to determine your target point, factoring in all the information you've been able to ascertain.

Putting Proper Pace on Your Putt

Once you've made a good read of your putt and chosen a starting target, you're ready to make your play. Take a practice stroke next to your ball while looking at the hole. This will program your mind for the length of the stroke you need. (Something you can do quickly before your practice stroke is to move your right arm back and forth as if you were going to toss the ball to the hole. This will give you some idea of how much arm swing you need. It works quite well.)

If you have an uphill putt, take your practice strokes from behind the ball. The more uphill and the longer the putt, the farther behind your ball you should stand. On downhill putts, stand closer to the hole than the position of your ball. In both cases, you'll be practicing a stroke for a putt from a distance on flat ground. The longer practice stroke you make from behind an uphill putt will allow for the hill. Same thing with the shorter practice stroke you make closer to the hole on a downhill putt.

When you make your stroke, pick out a single dimple on the ball and zero in on it. Keep your head steady and take the club back and through the same distance. You get your distance from how far you swing the putter back—the farther back you swing it, the farther the putt will go—but you don't get the true value of that distance unless you follow through to the same degree that you took the putter back.

9

THE
BIG
SWING
PRIMER

This book is mostly about making adjustments to your on-course thinking and game management, and about tweaking your shot selections and shot-making skills. The book assumes (it's a smart book!) that you were a player of some competence before you pulled it off the shelf in the bookstore. However, golf is a game filled with trade-offs: You start driving the ball well, and your putter goes south on you. You start putting well, but then you can't hit the ball close enough to the hole to have a reasonable putt. The big trade-off, of course, is that once a certain swing key starts to work for you, it stops working just as quickly. We realize that you're not going to run off to a teaching pro every time your swing goes ker-plooey on you. Instead you're going to try to fix it yourself. And to fix anything you have to understand the mechanics of it. In other words, you need the instructions for how it works. Use this swing primer as a reference source when you need to fix a broken swing.

Before You Even Swing the Club

The search for lower scores begins and is most critical during the process that occurs before the club even begins moving. More avoidable mistakes and more ball-flight inconsistencies arise as a result of miscues in *preparation* for swinging the club than as the result of anything that happens when the club is actually being swung. Trying to fix a mistake in midswing is simply not feasible, but trying to prevent the mistake before your swing has begun is a very attainable goal indeed. The good news is that properly setting up to the ball is a fairly simple process. Once you understand all the checkpoints, the biggest potential pitfall is getting careless in monitoring yourself as you set up to play a shot. The best way to avoid this is to have a pre-shot routine you go through before every shot you play with a full swing.

Placing Your Hands on the Club

With all the turning and shifting and gyrating your body does while swinging the club, it's sort of funny that your hands are the only parts of your body to come in contact with the club. The position of your hands on the club is the first fundamental that every golfer needs to fully understand, because once you start to swing, tremendous momentum begins to build up and the club is moving too fast for any type of grip correction to occur. If you do not position your hands perfectly on the club, you adversely affect the position of the clubface at impact, and when the clubface is off square by even the tiniest of margins, the resulting shot is exponentially off target.

Consider four things when you are positioning the club in your hands: where the club sits in your hands; whether your hands are in a *strong, weak,* or *neutral* position; how your hands work together; and the amount and placement of pressure on the club.

Place the Club in Your Fingers

When you are gripping the club, the shaft should rest in your fingers. Specifically, it should rest at the point where the fingers join your palm. The top of the shaft should rest against the fleshy, padded part of your left hand—what would be the lower right quadrant of your left palm if you held your hand up in front of your face. You never want to feel like the club is resting in your palms, because this will reduce your sense of feel of the weight of the clubhead and also hinder the action of your hands throughout the swing.

A Neutral, Weak, or Strong Grip

Once you are comfortable with the idea of the club resting mainly in your fingers, the next step is to position your left hand properly on the club. Actually, what we really want you to focus on is the position of your left thumb on the grip. If you place your thumb directly on top of the shaft so your thumb runs straight down the middle of the shaft, you are placing your hand in a neutral position. If you were to turn your hand (and your thumb) slightly to the right—say, one-quarter inch to one-half inch—you would be placing your hand in what is known as a strong position. If you did the opposite, and turned your hand and thumb so the thumb rested to the left of the center of the shaft, you would be setting a weak grip position. The obvious question is, "Which one is best for me?"

To answer that question, it helps to know what each of the three terms—neutral, strong, and weak—means.

- In the neutral position, the position of your left hand and thumb does not exert any extraneous influence on the angle of the clubface at impact. In other words, if you set the club-face square at address, took a neutral grip, and made a perfect swing, the clubface would be perfectly square at impact.
- In the strong position, with your left hand and thumb turned to the right of the center of the shaft, the tendency is for the clubface to be slightly *closed* at impact, even if you start from a square position at address. *Closed* refers to the idea that the lead edge of the club will be aimed left of your target.
- In the weak position, with your left thumb sitting slightly to the left of the center of the shaft, the tendency is for the club-face to be slightly open at impact. Again, this is true even if you have the clubface squarely aimed at address. When the clubface is open at impact the lead edge is pointing to the right of your target.

You can easily see the impact of each of these left hand/thumb positions without making a full swing. Pick up a club and turn your left hand so the thumb is on the right side of the shaft at the three-o'clock position. You don't even need your right hand on the club to do this. Swing the club back in slow motion, as if you were going to swing, and you will see immediately that the clubface turns down or, in effect, closes. With a strong grip and a real swing, this initial closing effect stays with the clubface through impact. Next, turn your left hand so the thumb is on the left side of the shaft. Repeat your slow-motion drill and you will get the sense of the club fanning up or open. With your thumb in the neutral position, you can move the club straight back from the ball without feeling that it wants to turn one way or the other.

Still, the question remains, "Which is the best way for me to grip the club?" The strong grip has a tendency to produce shots that curve from right to left—a ball-flight pattern that is considered ideal for most players. It also produces the most topspin, which means tee shots tend to run farther once they hit the ground. A weak grip generally produces shots that drift softly from left to right. A neutral grip has no effect on the flight of the ball. Throughout the history of the game, great players have employed each of these grips. Although each of the grip positions can work and do work for players of all levels, you should consider what the majority of good players do and what your needs are. A vast number of great players use a *slightly* strong grip—nowhere near as extreme as the one suggested in the above demonstration. They probably position the left thumb in approximately the one o'clock to one-thirty range. This moderately strong position helps to generate a slight draw and to create more roll when the ball hits the ground, but it is not so strong as to create problems for most players.

For the typical weekend player who is continually striving for more distance, a moderately strong grip is probably best. If you consistently hit off-line shots in the same pattern, checking your grip might be the place to start the cure. Consistently wild hooks could be caused by an excessively strong grip, whereas frequent wild slices may be the result of a weak grip.

What about the neutral grip? If you feel your swing mechanics are so sound that you can repeatedly reach the impact position with the clubface perfectly square, it's a valid option. Otherwise, if you are a tad erratic, the moderately strong grip at least allows you to develop a predominant ball flight.

The Hands Working as a Unit

With all the emphasis that has been placed on the left hand, you might think that your right hand has nothing to do with your golf swing. As you probably already know, that's not true. Because the left hand is placed on the club first and because it also dictates the position of the right hand, it always precedes the right hand in any discussion of grip.

To swing the club most effectively you need both hands to work together as a complementary unit. There are a few ways to accomplish this. The two main ways are the overlapping or Vardon grip, and the interlocking grip. Both grips start by placing the "V" of the right palm and, as a result, the right thumb, over the top of the left thumb. In the overlapping/Vardon grip, the union of the hands is completed by placing the right pinkie finger directly on top of the left index finger. Some players choose to place the right pinkie finger in the crease between the left index finger and the left middle finger.

With the interlocking grip you take the notion of coupling the hands literally by looping the right pinkie finger through the gap between the left index finger and the left middle finger.

The overlapping grip and the interlocking grip are the two most commonly used grips, but an overwhelming majority of top-level players use the overlapping grip. There are some notable exceptions, such as Jack Nicklaus and Tom Kite. Some everyday golfers who have fingers on the short side prefer the interlocking as well, because it gives them a more solid sense of connection between the two hands.

Once you have both hands on the club, one classic tip for checking the position of your hands is this: The "V" formed by the left thumb and index finger should point at your left shoulder. The "V" formed by the right thumb and index finger should point at your right shoulder.

Paying Attention to How Hard You Squeeze the Club

We used the word *squeeze* in that little headline to get your attention, but the fact is we don't want you thinking about squeezing the club because you'll probably squeeze too hard, as you do with the Charmin. There is little question that the everyday golfer squeezes the club too tightly and that this has a negative influence on performance. The downside of squeezing the club is twofold: It reduces your sense of feel for the clubhead, and it creates tension in your arms, restricting freedom of movement during the swing. These are both significant drawbacks because it is essential to have a sense of where the clubhead is at all points during the swing, and tension in any form turns the swing into more of a whack or hack, replacing fluidity with lumberjack swings.

There are really only two things to think about when it comes to grip pressure: how much to apply and where to apply it. How much pressure you apply is the more important of the two, and the answer is that you should hold the club as lightly as possible. Apply only enough grip pressure to keep the club from flying out of your hands when you swing. If you can feel any tension at all in your forearms, you are squeezing the club way too hard. An image that works well is to think of holding something rather soft in your hands as you grip the club.

Where you apply the pressure is something that happens quite naturally based on the way you grip the club. For the most part, the top three fingers on your left hand (pinkie, ring finger, and middle finger) apply the most significant amount of pressure. On your right hand you squeeze mainly with two fingers, the middle and ring fingers. Knowing where to apply the pressure is useful only to the extent that when you are trying for the lightest possible grip, it helps to know where you should feel the pressure.

PLAY A SHOT LIKE AN ATHLETE INSTEAD OF AN ACCOUNTANT

Once you've settled on a grip that feels good to you, the next step in swinging a golf club is to put your body into a position that will allow it to move in an uninhibited manner. The word typically applied to this element of preparing to play a shot is *posture*, but it helps to think in terms of assuming an athletic position. (*Posture* makes most people think simply of the angle of the back, but setting your body to swing a golf club involves more than that.)

There is a universal athletic position that applies to nearly every sport, including golf. That position consists of the following things: the feet spread apart for balance and the body weight evenly distributed on the balls of both feet, the knees flexed, the upper body angled forward from the hips, the arms hanging loose and free of tension, and the head steady at the center. If this position does not *sound* familiar to you, it should at least look familiar. It is the position a linebacker takes as he prepares for the snap of the ball; it is the position of a tennis player awaiting service; it is, with the exception of the arms hanging down, the position a baseball player takes when awaiting a pitch; it is the position a basketball player takes just before shooting a free throw. In a more extreme form, it is the position a swimmer takes on the starting blocks waiting for the gun to sound. What do all of these examples have in common? Each athlete assumes this position while waiting for the action to begin. They are not simply waiting, however. They are preparing themselves to react quickly and smoothly to the action. This state of preparedness is just as vital as the action itself. Here are the key points in taking an athletic stance:

- A solid base, which means your feet are separated and your weight is evenly balanced between both feet. The basic reference point for how wide to spread your feet is your shoulders. For a full shot played with your driver, the insides of your feet should be approximately the width of your shoulders. The width between your feet narrows as the clubs (and your swing) get shorter. However, your shoulders always serve as the reference points.

- Your weight should be toward the balls of your feet, but not so much that you tip forward as you stand ready to play a shot. You also want to be careful not to get so much weight toward the rear of your feet that you feel as if you are falling backward as you stand ready to swing. The key is to feel balanced.

- Flex your knees; this reduces tension and allows your lower body to do what it needs to do. Flexing the knees also helps to lower the clubhead to the ball without compromising the angle of your back and shoulders—that is, it allows you to reach the ball without slouching your shoulders. How far should you bend your knees? If you picture a line from the side of the ball of your foot going straight up—perpendicular to the ground—it should go directly through the center of the side of your knee. If it helps, draw that mental line while you are standing straight, and you will get a sense of how much you should flex your knees.

- Your arms should hang straight down and be tension free. Even with your knees flexed and your arms hanging down and free of tension, however, your hands would still be too close to your body to swing freely and allow full extension of your arms. To create enough separation between your hands and body, bend forward slightly from your hips while keeping your back straight. In this sense, "straight" means that, as you bend forward from the hips, you are careful not to droop your shoulders. How far forward from your hips should you bend? Think of the line that started straight up from the ball of your foot and through the center of your knee. If you continue that line straight up from the knee until the point where it goes directly through the center of the side of your armpit, you should be close to getting the correct amount of flex forward from your hips.

- Your head should be set in a position that allows you to see what is happening. You want to avoid dropping your chin down onto your chest just because the ball is on the ground. You must tilt your head down a tiny bit to see the ball, but don't tip it down any farther than necessary to see the ball. It helps to remember that your left shoulder must pass under your chin during a full swing, and that is not possible if your chin is on your chest.

Accurately Aiming Your Body and the Club

Just as in any other target game, your accuracy in golf depends on how well you aim. In almost every game that requires proper aim, the main element of the aiming process is the alignment of your body to the target. Once your body is in proper relationship to the target, you have won most of the aiming battle. The second element is properly aiming your club. Aiming your body and your club to play a shot consists of two separate parts: the checkpoints of proper body and club alignment, and the sequence of events required to achieve these checkpoints most effectively. You must first understand the aiming checkpoints for the body/target relationship before moving on to the sequence of events in setting up to play a shot.

There are numerous variables in choosing your target for a given shot, all of which are mentioned in the early chapters of this book. The one absolute is that the target for a shot played with a full swing—actually any swing other than your putting stroke—is always the spot you want the ball to first strike the ground. Where the ball runs to after it strikes the ground, or what it does while in the air, are irrelevant to the selection of your target.

For almost every shot you play with a full swing—especially as it relates to this fundamental discussion—the lead edge of the club should be aimed directly at the target. The lead edge is the straight edge where the clubface and the sole of the club join. In other words, from the lead edge of the clubface, a straight line—perpendicular to the lead edge—extends to your target. A straight line running from the lead edge of the club to the target is the target line.

Aiming your body is perhaps the most difficult part of getting set to play a shot. Because you are standing to the side of the ball, and because you are not aiming your body at the target, it is not uncommon for some visual confusion to occur. This is complicated because you are not, at least in the final address position, looking at the target with both eyes.

The alignment of your body is related to the alignment of your clubface. More specifically, the alignment of your body is related to the target line, the straight line from the clubface to the target. The key thing to remember about aiming is *not* to aim your body directly at the target. Aim your body along a line parallel to the target line.

The idea of aiming your body parallel to the target line is important. If you aimed your body directly at the target, it would create problems in your swing. Here, however, it is best to consider exactly how to aim your body.

When you aim the clubface at the target, you have a reference point: the leading edge of the clubface. You have reference points for aiming your body, too. Specifically, your feet, hips, and shoulders form the lines that you set parallel to the target line. The basic reference for a fundamentally sound setup is as follows: A straight line across the tips of your toes, a straight line from hip to hip, and a straight line from shoulder to shoulder should all be parallel to your target line.

You might wonder how, if you aim your clubface directly at your target and aim your body at a point left of (but parallel to) your target, the ball ends up where you want it. Some simple visualization can put this into perspective. At the center of this discussion of alignment stand two straight lines that run parallel to each other from the ball to (and beyond) your target. The line farthest from you—which extends from the clubface and the ball to the target—is your target line. The other line is formed by your body: those straight lines across your toes, your hips, and your shoulders. You can think of these as your body lines. For a moment, think of these two lines as the two rails on a railroad track. Don't visualize this from the perspective of your address position next to the ball. Rather visualize it from a vantage point behind the ball. In other words, the ball is directly between you and your target. As you mentally picture yourself standing between the two rails, you will see that the farther you look down the line, the closer the two rails appear to be. Eventually the two rails visually merge into a single rail or a single line. This is precisely the way you need to consider aiming your club and your body: They travel along different lines, but they eventually come together at a common destination.

"Stepping" into Your Setup Position

Many of the difficulties people encounter playing golf arise because of the ball-to-body-to-target orientation. Properly aiming your club and body depends heavily on your grasp of a series of straight lines. In golf, the straight lines appear straight only if you observe them from directly behind the ball. This is where you are at a disadvantage in golf, because you are not behind the ball as you play it. You can, however, properly aim yourself and the club by following a certain sequence of events, one that allows you to gain orientation to the target from behind the ball before you move around to the side of the ball to swing the club. The start of that sequence of events begins like everything else in golf—with the selection of a target.

Exactly which point you pick as a target varies from shot to shot and from club to club, because you must consider what the ball will do once it strikes the ground—an often overlooked aspect of playing a shot. The ball reacts differently depending on the angle at which it strikes the ground. The steeper the angle at which the ball hits the ground, the less it rolls once it has landed. Remember, however, that for aiming purposes your target is always the point at which you wish the ball to hit the ground. Where the ball will stop is not a consideration in aiming your body.

One of the few rules of golf that you should never violate is this: *Always decide on your target from a point behind the ball.* In fact (reverting to the straight lines again), while deciding on a target for your shot, you should be standing behind the ball on a straight line that runs from the target to (and through) your ball.

Here is a step-by-step breakdown of the process of selecting a target and aligning your body to that target:

- Before you select a club, stand behind the ball and get acquainted with the shot you are about to play. If that shot is played from the tee box, you know you are going to have a good lie because you should tee the ball up for every tee shot. For any other shot, the first thing you should do is assess the lie of the ball. This is important; you cannot decide on your target (or your club) until you have assessed the lie of your ball. If the lie is clean—there is no long grass around the ball, it is not in a divot, and the ground is relatively flat—you can safely assume it won't affect your shot much.

- Once you are sure that the lie will not affect your shot very much, you can select a target. At this point you are standing behind the ball and looking down the line toward your eventual destination. At this moment you should be thinking about three things: your actual target; a landmark in the distance beyond that target (if there is one); and, most important, an intermediate target—that is, a spot between your actual target and your ball. You should be very precise in selecting a target. You should not think, "I'm sort of aiming at that," or "I want to hit this one in that general direction." You should choose a specific spot on the ground toward which you wish to play the shot.
- Once you pick your target, you return to those straight lines. Because the ball is rather tiny and your target is rather far away, it can be difficult to put the two—the small ball and the faraway small target—into perspective. Therefore, it is a good idea to pick a big target that lies beyond your actual target— for example, a tree, bush, hill, building or anything that lies on a direct line beyond your target.
- Now that you've selected your big target, you can greatly increase your chances of accurately aiming your club and yourself by selecting an intermediate target, a point that is closer to you but along the same line as the big target. How do you do that? The answer is more lines. Mentally draw a straight line from your ball to your big target. Along that line select something on the ground within three feet of your ball. It can be anything—a twig, a leaf, a discolored patch of grass, a divot, a piece of clover, anything that will serve as a visual reference. Selecting an intermediate target is the most important thing you do in preparing to play a shot.
- You have done all of the above while standing behind the ball. While you are still standing behind the ball, make a visual connection (draw a straight line) from your ball to your

intermediate target to your actual target. The reason the intermediate target should be as close as possible to the ball is that
it is the point at which you aim your clubface. Once you aim
your clubface, you can set your body in place as well.

- Now you start to move into position. As you move up next to
  the ball, you step into the setup position with your right foot
  first, keeping your head and shoulders directly facing your target. You do this so you can aim the club while you are looking at your target with both eyes. This keeps you from peering
  at the target out of the corner of your left eye, which is quite
  often disorienting.
- You aim your club by setting the lead edge square (perpendicular) to your target line. At this point you should be comfortable with your target line, because you have selected the
  intermediate target close to the ball. Aim your club directly at
  the intermediate target. Setting the club on the ground behind
  the ball makes things simpler, and it helps reduce the amount
  of tension in your arms.
- Once you have aimed the club, you can step into your setup
  position with your left side. Because the club is already aimed,
  you can concentrate on making your body lines parallel to
  your target line. It is easiest to start with your feet, because
  they are closest to the target line. Next set your shoulders parallel to the target line. Once your feet and shoulders are set,
  you have accomplished what you need to do to aim your club
  and body. Now it is simply a matter of assuming the athletic
  position described earlier.
- Once the club is set, the shaft should be leaning slightly
  toward the target, with your hands slightly ahead of the clubhead. At the very least, your hands should be even with the
  clubhead and the shaft should be straight. You never want to
  be in a position where your hands are behind the clubhead or
  the shaft is leaning away from the target.

How to Swing That Thing

There is no precise moment when your pre-swing ends and the swing itself begins. In a similar vein, there is no clear delineation between the end of your backswing and the beginning of the forward swing (downswing). It is not important to know when one portion of the swing begins and ends. It is a package: One thing leads directly into the next. The choice of a target leads into the approach to the ball; your approach to the ball leads to a proper setup; a proper setup leads into the beginning of your backswing; the backswing transitions to the downswing, which leads to impact, which ends in the follow-through. It is all related. The first few inches of the club's movement in your backswing are referred to as the takeaway. The first 18 to 24 inches set the tone for the remainder of the swing. The swing itself is a blur, started and finished in the blink of an eye. That is why the pre-shot and early phases of the swing are so important. Once you set the process in motion, there is no time to think and react.

Beginning Your Backswing

One of the keys to a good swing is to focus on the idea that it is indeed a swing. Golfers of all levels sometimes lose sight of this and think about the idea of hitting the ball. You should always think of the movement of the club as a swing of the clubhead. In other words, your body movements combine to swing the clubhead. No matter how many movements you make or how many things are going on, the goal is to swing the clubhead and (this is important) maintain your sense of connection to the clubhead while swinging it. Always "feel" the clubhead while it is being swung. You never want to feel like you're swinging the shaft—a stiff feeling akin to swinging a baseball bat.

One of the keys to maintaining this feeling of connection to the clubhead can be found in the takeaway, those vital first inches of the clubhead's movement. During the takeaway, the only way to maintain a sense of feeling of the clubhead is to keep tension—particularly in your upper body—to a minimum. To minimize tension, maintain subtle movements of the body from the early phases of your setup right through to the beginning of your swing.

A second key to maintaining a unified feeling of body and clubhead is to monitor grip pressure, as we mentioned earlier in this primer.

The final major key to maintaining the feel for your clubhead is to make all the body movements of the swing at the same tempo. Tempo does not refer to how fast you swing the club. Rather, tempo refers to the consistency of the pace at which you swing the club. In other words, it doesn't matter how fast or how slow you swing the club, as long as the pace of the swing is consistent.

You may wonder why a section dealing with takeaway is discussing tempo. The critical first inches of your swing are the time to make the biggest stride toward ensuring a consistent tempo. If you start moving the club away slowly and smoothly, you have an excellent chance of maintaining the same tempo throughout your swing.

The idea of starting the club away slowly may raise another question: "If I start the club away slowly, how am I ever going to make the club move fast enough to crush the ball in the manner that a massively strong bull like me should?" The answer is that the club will pick up speed even though your body is moving at the same tempo throughout your swing. This idea is covered more thoroughly below. For the moment, however, you need to know only that it does in fact work out that way. For the time being, however, we should focus on the takeaway.

Why does a slow, smooth takeaway help your tempo? When you start the club away slowly and smoothly, you have started it at a pace that is both manageable and easy to keep free of tension. When you take the club away from the ball quickly you will inevitably squeeze the grip with your hands and increase tension in your arms. Why? Remember that to maintain the feel of the clubhead, you want to have a minimal amount of grip pressure. When you are gripping the club lightly, any sudden jerking of the club requires you to squeeze tighter to prevent the club from flying out of your hands. The more you squeeze, the more tension you create.

The takeaway is not only the best opportunity for setting the club in motion at a manageable pace. It is also the best chance to get the club started on the proper path. Here the word *path* refers to the movement of the clubhead throughout your swing. Ideally, the club will travel on the longest possible (widest) path throughout your swing because the longer the arc of the swing, the more speed it will build up, increasing the distance the ball will travel.

You want the club to remain on a path that will return it to the ball from an angle just inside the target line. (The club does not travel along the target line—a straight line—for very long because you swing the club around your body.) Following this path provides the best chance of the clubhead's being square at impact. To keep the club on this path all the way to impact is a challenge, but it is almost impossible to accomplish if you don't start the club away from the ball on a straight line for as long as possible—that is, until your arms are extended to such a point that they start to swing up rather than back. If you start your swing by immediately moving the club off the initial straight-back path—to either the outside or the inside—you dramatically reduce your chances of hitting a straight shot. Therefore, take the club away from the ball slowly so you can keep it in a straight line for as long as possible. The quicker you jerk the club back, the more likely you are to move it off the path you want—most likely too far to the inside. Taking the club back outside the target line—moving the clubhead away from your body—is not ideal either.

Here are the two basic characteristics of a solid takeaway: It should be slow, and the club should move straight back from the ball for as long as possible. These two characteristics produce a number of desirable results, but how do you go about setting the club in motion to achieve them?

You should slide into the actual movement of the club from some preliminary movement that helps you to stay loose—a waggle, some jiggling of the feet, a forward press of the hands, or perhaps a combination of these things. Once you pull your swing trigger, however, what are the checkmarks you should be looking for?

One of the most common and effective ways of visualizing the takeaway is what is commonly referred to as the one-piece takeaway. Here is how it works: The lines of your arms, from your shoulders to your hands, form a triangle. We'll call it an upside-down triangle, meaning that the base of the triangle—bottom part—runs between your shoulders, and the top point of it comes together at your hands. For the initial movements of your swing, that triangle stays intact. The club moves along with it, an extension of the line formed by your left arm. Later in your swing, the triangle breaks down: Your right elbow bends, your body has turned, and the shaft of the club is no longer in a straight line with your left arm. At the outset of your swing, however, the idea of the triangle, along with the club, starting away from the ball all at once and together, is extremely useful.

Another way of visualizing the takeaway is to think of *keeping the left arm straight as you move the club back* from the ball and as it swings up and across your chest. Remember those great key words, "low and slow." They can be helpful when you are struggling with your swing.

A caution: Don't take this visual image of a triangle too literally. Don't force your arms to be straight lines, to be absolutely rigid. The visual image of the triangle is meant only to give you a mental snapshot of how the body parts and the club work together. Remember your setup keys: arms hang relaxed, grip pressure is light. You are not a machine—or even a triangle, for that matter—so don't try to swing like one.

As noted, the triangle eventually breaks down. If you are too rigid as you move away from the ball, you will not be able to move successfully into the following phases of the swing.

Okay, I Have This Thing Moving. Now What the Hell Do I Do?

Soon after the clubhead begins to move, other things happen. In fact, they happen so soon after the clubhead begins to move that they occur nearly simultaneously. You don't have to force them to happen. Many result from a good setup and the takeaway notions described above.

You may be wondering, "If that's the case, why bother telling me about them? Why confuse me with a bunch of stuff that will just happen anyway?" The reason is that, at any given time during a round or a part of your season, your sense of what you are doing can vanish, and shots can start flying all over the place. You don't know what to do, and the only solution seems to be banging your head against a wall until you're unconscious and simply unable to worry about your golf game. Trust us, we've tried that and it really hurts. We'd rather you try using some solid swing keys to get yourself back on track. Swing keys are nuggets of information that can help you fix your swing. The deal is that you think about only one thing and it frees your mind of clutter and lets your body do the work. The majority of swing keys lie buried in the reflexive actions of the swing. The things you don't need to think about when things are going well can be your savior in your hours of need.

During the takeaway, your left shoulder starts to move toward your chin. Eventually your shoulder will feel like it is under your chin, which is why your chin should not droop on your chest at address. Don't turn your head during your backswing to make room for your shoulder. Nothing could be more disorienting, which is why the head position at address is so important. (One of Jack Nicklaus's trademark moves is the cocking of his head—his chin turns slightly to his right—just before he begins to swing. This serves many purposes: It acts as a trigger for his swing, provides room for his huge shoulder turn, and allows him to keep his head steady.)

A split second after the club first moves, your hips and shoulders begin to turn. This movement plays a vital role in the production of clubhead speed, which results in power.

Finally your weight—which was equally distributed between your feet at address—now shifts so that much of it is on your right leg, more specifically the inside of your right leg and foot. To accommodate this, many players kick the left knee toward the right in the backswing, lifting the left heel slightly off the ground, or rolling the entire left foot onto the instep. If this feels good to you, do it. Just remember that the left knee should never jut out toward the target line. Rather, it kicks in toward your right knee.

At a certain point, it becomes impossible for the club to continue straight back from the ball. It does not matter precisely where that point is—it is the result of your hips and shoulders turning away from the ball. Because the turning movement of your hips and shoulders is of major importance in your swing, it is important that you understand exactly what turn means and exactly how your hips and shoulders turn.

When your arms make that first movement, they are swinging as far back as they can unaided significantly by any additional body movement. You would not be able to hit the ball very far if this were the only movement involved in your swing. Of course, it isn't the only movement.

Most of the turning of your shoulders and hips occurs simultaneously. Your hips may start turning away from the ball just a hair before your shoulders do, but it does not really matter. The turning of your hips and shoulders is responsible for generating the power in your swing. Think of your swing as the coiling and uncoiling of a spring.

For a spring to coil, at least one end of it must be fixed so that the spring has something to resist against. The same is true of your swing. During the backswing, the inside of your right leg and foot serve as this fixed point, which is where you should feel most of your weight. Your hips and shoulders turn around that fixed point in your right leg. The turning continues until your shoulders have turned approximately twice as much as your hips have. At what is considered the top of your swing, your hips should have turned roughly 45 degrees from the point at which they started and your shoulders should have turned roughly 90 degrees from the point at which they started. These numbers are presented simply to give you an idea of the difference in the turning. It is not important to turn exactly 45 and 90 degrees. How far you can turn involves many factors: How naturally flexible you are, how old you are, your physical condition, etc.

Eventually your hips reach a point where they cannot turn any farther. At this point the shoulders continue turning away from the ball, tightening and tightening that spring until they have turned as far as they can.

How do you know when your hips and shoulders have reached the point of maximum turn? They just won't move any farther; you have reached your physical limits. There is something quite important to consider, however: The turning of the hips and shoulders must be parallel with the ground. In other words, your body must not tilt either to the left (most common in the backswing) or to the right (most common in the downswing). If you maintain and work on this idea of turning level to the ground, your body will let you know when you have made your maximum turn. You do want to make your maximum turn, because the farther you turn, the more power you will eventually release on the ball.

The great teacher Percy Boomer best described the turning of the hips as "turning in a barrel." What he meant by that was to imagine swinging the club with a wooden barrel around your legs, rising up to your hips. The image of the barrel does two things: It reminds you to keep your hips level with the top of the barrel, and it inhibits lateral motion in favor of the turning action. Ideally you should have very little lateral movement in your swing, which is why you concentrate on keeping your weight on the inside of your right leg and foot. If the weight shifts to the outside of the leg, you will sway laterally away from the ball.

During this turning, your arms have continued swinging back along with your shoulders. In fact, your arms are doing a bit of turning of their own, spinning in a clockwise direction. This spinning of your arms happens without conscious effort and is not something you need to think about. Your right elbow has also bent quite a bit by the time you reach the top of your swing. It starts to fold on its own as the club moves behind you. In addition, your wrists have cocked, as they must to lift the weight of the clubhead and support it at the top of your swing. If you keep your grip pressure light throughout your swing, you will instinctively cock and uncock your wrists. All of this happens while your hips and shoulders are turning, culminating in the moment known as the top or, more accurately, the transition phase of your swing.

The Big Switch from Backswing to Downswing

When everything during your backswing falls into place with the right timing, you reach a sweet spot in time—a moment of suspended animation when everything seems to hover motionless for just the tiniest fraction of a second before the club starts down toward the ball. This moment, called the pause at the top, is incredibly vital to your swing. Here is what happens.

After your hips have finished turning—when they cannot move any farther and still remain level with the ground—your shoulders keep moving. In essence, your hips are ready to be cut loose, but they have to wait for the shoulder turn to finish. More precisely, you must wait for your shoulder turn to finish. When it does, you want to feel a pause in the movement of your upper body for just a microsecond. Why? Because this tightly wound spring has already begun to unwind the way you want it to—from the bottom (the fixed point)—up. That split-second pause—which is almost imperceptible if you are swinging with a nice tempo—gives your lower body a chance to get the proper head start on the way down, which is exactly what you want to happen. As you approach that moment when your shoulders shift from turning back to turning through, your hips have already started their forward swing. This brief pause at the top allows a few hugely beneficial things to happen.

First, it allows your upper body to be pulled along by the lower body. Reverting to the spring analogy, the lower body is where the most energy is stored up, so you want the upper body to hang back a fraction of a second until it is whipped forward by the unwinding of the lower body.

Second, the pause at the top allows you to make sure you begin the downswing by keeping your hips and shoulders level, just as they were when they were going back. This helps prevent you from making one of golf's most classic mistakes: swinging over the top, or thrusting the right shoulder out toward the target line in an effort that is perceived as powerful (but is in fact a power leak) and that causes all sorts of horrible-looking shots.

Third, the pause makes it less likely that you will increase your grip pressure at the top, something that is frequently referred to as regripping. This happens most often when the upper body transition is not smooth but is rather a hurried, out-of-control sequence. The sudden shift in tempo causes you to hang on in an effort to control the club.

Fourth, the pause gives you a moment to feel the planting of your left foot and the shift to the left leg as the fixed point in your swing. As you swing the club back—away from your target—you pivot around your back (right) leg. As you begin the forward swing, you must switch the pivot point to your front (left) leg because you simply cannot swing to and through the ball with all your weight remaining on your right leg; you would probably fall backward. The moment your upper body starts to unwind, most of your weight switches to your left leg and foot. This weight shift will solidly plant your left foot on the ground until well after impact.

Two key yet distinct checkpoints are often used to judge the position of the club at the top of your swing: the position of your club in relation to the ground, and the position of your left wrist. These two things are important because you cannot see the club (we all wish we could!) and because all will go well in the downswing if you have the club set properly at the top of your swing.

You may have heard that the shaft of the club should be parallel to the ground at the top of the swing. More than anything else, the position of the shaft is a common reference point for marking what is considered a controlled swing—that is, to swing past the point where the shaft is parallel to the ground would indicate a swing so excessive that it is impossible to maintain balance and timing, etc. It is also commonly deemed the point you must reach to have made a backswing sufficiently long enough to generate any power. The first part of the parallel theory—that to go beyond parallel is to be out of control—doesn't hold water. The young Jack Nicklaus, Bobby Jones and many other extremely long, accurate strikers of the ball took the club well beyond parallel. The second part—to come short of parallel indicates a deficiency of power—is also a bit flimsy. Some very long hitters have backswings that come up well short of parallel. The crux of the matter is that you can turn as far as your body allows if you can swing with enough strength to control the coiling throughout and can wait at the top to let things proceed in order.

The position of your left wrist, however, is very important. Because the purpose of your swing is to deliver the clubface squarely to the ball, it would be nice if you had some way of knowing the position of the clubface at the top of your swing. Assuming you are using a basically neutral grip, your left wrist should be flat at the top of your swing—that is, it should not bend. If your wrist is flat, you know the clubface is still square. If it is cupped so that the back of your left hand is directly facing you, the clubface is closed. If it is bowed so that the back of your left hand is facing directly toward the sky, the clubface is open.

Much ado is made of swinging the golf club and the arms on a level plane throughout the entire golf swing, a notion made popular by Ben Hogan. Although a consistently planed swing is the hallmark of many great players, it is not an event unto itself. It is the result of doing many other things correctly. In other words, don't worry about it. If you turn level, and if you consistently feel like the clubface is square at the top of your swing, you are in good shape.

RETURNING THE CLUB TO THE BALL

Once you have made a smooth transition (think tempo— there's no reason for you to feel as if you are quickening your swing) and planted your left foot, your hips move forward toward your target, and your upper body catches up. You might think of it as a race that finishes in a dead heat. Even though your upper body trails behind at the start of the downswing, it gains speed as it moves without your trying to move any faster. The result is that the club—by extension the farthest point of the spring from the fixed end—receives all the energy and begins to move at ever-increasing speed until impact.

The sequence of events happens so fast on the downswing that, practically speaking, once you have set your weight on your left leg, have planted your left foot, and have made it through the transition phase without rushing to "hit at" the ball, you have done all you can to affect what happens next.

Aside from a bit of flex in the knee, your left leg is firm, presenting the strongest possible fixed point against which your coil can unleash. If you have maintained your posture throughout your swing and have turned level away from the ball, the club should be on the desired path for square impact. The club will approach the ball on a curved line that begins slightly inside the target line, runs directly along the target line for a brief flash—impact!—and then extends down the target line before swinging up and around your body.

As you near impact, both arms are fully extended, and at the crucial moment of impact the back of your left hand is directly facing your target. Your arms extend on their own as a result of all the force being generated—it is not a conscious movement as long as you are not standing too close to the ball. (Likewise, the turning of your hands through impact is part and parcel of the release of power. There should not be a conscious turning of the right hand over the left through impact. Such a movement usually leads to a flawed shot.) Once your arms are fully extended, the clubhead makes its final amazing acceleration and catches up to your hands at impact. Your hips have turned vigorously so that they are not parallel to the target line but have begun to face or turn toward the target, on their way to their final follow-through position. This may seem like a brief description of the downswing, but the downswing is really a reaction to what you have started with your setup and backswing. The biggest key is patience.

THE FOLLOW-THROUGH: PAUSE ON IT JUST LIKE THE PROS DO

If you have played or watched golf for any length of time, you have probably heard the expressions "He quit on it" or "He didn't finish his swing." What exactly does that mean? It means that to get the full positive effect of everything you have done leading up to impact, you must swing just as vigorously through the ball as you did before striking it. When you slow down through the ball or just slap at it, the chances of the clubface's being square at impact are greatly reduced. If, on the other hand, you are able to complete a full, balanced follow-through, you have done a lot of things correctly.

Like the other parts of your swing, your follow-through blends into the part of the swing preceding it, the downswing and impact. Impact is such a fleeting moment that what you do afterward runs into what you did before.

The first stage of your follow-through is set early in your downswing. Once you have set the weight on your left leg, you have set the pivot point around which the rest of your swing will turn. After you have hit the ball, you will still be turning around your left leg.

The first active stage of your follow-through starts when your arms are fully extended through the impact zone. In fact, after impact, you should fully extend your arms for as long as possible. Think about pushing with the right arm and pulling with the left arm, or driving the clubhead toward the target for as long as possible. Because you are making a round swing, you cannot keep the clubhead moving along the target line for very long, but you should feel as if you are moving the clubhead directly for the target for as long as possible. That full, long extension will help you reap the rewards of power you prepared for in your backswing and downswing.

At the same time, you should be forcefully turning your right hip through toward the target (again, driving is a good word to describe it).

After you have reached full extension in your follow-through, your right shoulder will start to turn your head upward so you can watch the flight of the ball. Until this point in your swing, your head should remain steady.

As the club swings toward the conclusion of your swing, you should be thinking about your hands finishing the swing somewhere in the area next to your left ear. That's how far you should swing the club before you think of your swing as finished. When you reach this point your weight should be balanced on your left leg, and your entire body should be facing the target. Have you noticed how professionals pose on a shot after striking it? Or perhaps you have caught yourself or a friend doing it after a very fine shot? That's exactly how you should finish every full swing you make.

10

Preparing
Your Body
to Play

I t defies mathematics to calculate the number of potentially good rounds of golf that have been spoiled because a player wasn't loose before he or she went to the first tee. That's never going to happen to you again because you're going to read and act on this very brief chapter. Besides, we promised you earlier in the book we'd tell you this stuff.

Pre-Round, Pre-Practice
Tee Stretching

Okay, you made it to the golf course without driving into a tree. Congratulations. We're very proud of you. Now what? Instead of hanging around the grillroom shooting the breeze, get yourself ready to play. Start with these stretches.

- Turn your head to the right, looking as far over your shoulder as possible. Now take your left hand and push gently against the left side of your face. (Careful, now. Don't shove your own head.) Hold this for 15 seconds. Switch sides, and repeat for a total of three times with each side of your head.
- Reach across your body with your left arm and grab the back of your right elbow with your left hand. Now pull your right arm across your body, getting your right shoulder under your chin if you can. Hold for 10 seconds, then switch arms. Repeat for a total of three times with each arm.
- Clasp your hands behind your back and raise your arms up and back. Inhale to increase the stretch. Do this three times, holding it until you feel some looseness.
- Bend forward *slowly* from your waist and grasp your ankles. If you need to bend your knees, that's fine. If you can't reach your ankles, slide your hands down your legs as far as you can. Do this for 10 seconds, then raise yourself back up slowly. Do it two more times.
- Stand with your back up against a tree or a golf cart. Rotate your upper body to the right (without moving your feet) and grab onto the tree or cart or doorway or locker or whatever. Look over your left shoulder as you do this. Hold for 10 seconds, and repeat each side three times.
- Stand with your feet shoulder-width apart and raise your right arm above your head, reaching your hand toward the sky. Keeping your knees flexed, lean to your left and run your left hand down the outside of your left thigh, toward your knee. Hold for 10 seconds, then try the other side. Repeat three times.

HEAD FOR THE PRACTICE TEE

Now that you're all stretched out, head for the practice tee. Don't forget your clubs. Once you get there . . .

- Take a club out of your bag, and starting out very slowly make a continuous series of swings without stopping. Start from your address position and just keep swinging the club back and forth without stopping to reset your address position. You don't need a ball, and don't rush. You can add more speed to the swings as you get loose. Do this for about a minute.
- Take a pile of balls and start making progressively longer swings. Using your sand wedge, hit the first few balls about 20 yards or so. After you hit three balls, hit the next three 10 yards farther out. After you've hit about 15 balls, hit a few full wedges. Don't worry about making clean contact. If it bums you out to chunk a few, put the balls on a tee as you hit them.
- Head to the practice green and roll a few putts and get a feel for the greens. What's that you say? How come you didn't hit 300 balls on the range before you headed to the putting green? The reason is that pre-round preparation is about getting loose, not overhauling your swing. If you want to beat balls, do it after the round or during a separate practice session. For now, you're ready. Go get 'em. And when you break 90, the first beer is on us.

INDEX